THE BIG BOOK OF
THAI CURRIES

THE BIG BOOK OF
THAI CURRIES

VATCHARIN BHUMICHITR

Photography by **Martin Brigdale**
and **Somchai Phongphaisarnkit**

Kyle Cathie Limited

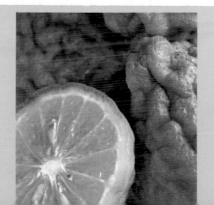

For my sister

First published in Great Britain in 2007 by
Kyle Cathie Limited
www.kylecathie.com

10 9 8 7 6 5 4 3 2

ISBN 978-1-85626-808-0

The publishers would like to thank Johnny Acton for his help.

Project editor **Jennifer Wheatley**
Designer **Fran Rawlinson**
Photographer **Martin Brigdale** and **Somchai Phongphaisarnkit**
Food styling **Annie Rigg** (apart from pages 97, 116, 123, 132, 135, 149, 169; **Linda Tubby**)
Styling **Helen Trent**
Copy editor **Stephanie Evans** and **Vanessa Kendell**
Editorial assistant **Vicki Murrell**
Production **Sha Huxtable** and **Alice Holloway**

A Cataloguing In Publication record for this title is available from the British Library.

Printed in China

CONTENTS

6 Introduction

9   Curries and Thai cooking

10   What is Thai cooking?

12   The role of curry in a Thai meal

15   Composition of a Thai curry

19   Regional differences

20   Making a Thai curry

22   Curry paste ingredients

24   Liquid ingredients

26   Making curry pastes

28   Curry paste recipes

32   Accompaniments

34   Pickles

36 Snacks and One-Dish Meals

64 Poultry

92 Meat

118 Fish

144 Vegetables and Fruit

172   Conversion table

173   Index

INTRODUCTION

'KIN KHAO LUA LANG!'

This is the traditional greeting you will hear all over Thailand. Unlike Western greetings, it doesn't mean 'how are you?' or 'hello'. It means 'have you eaten yet?'. This shows just how central food is to the Thai way of life. If the reply is no, the greeting will often be followed by an invitation to eat. And for a group of Thais sitting down to a meal, the first question is invariably 'kin gaeng arai dee?' or 'what curry shall we eat?'. The type of curry (green, red, yellow, etc.) and the kind of meat or fish to go in it are discussed first. Only when this is decided will the conversation turn to other elements of the meal – the stir-fries or steamed dishes and their respective ingredients.

curries and thai cooking

I always feel lucky to have been born in Thailand. The country is very fertile, irrigated as it is by the great Chao Phraya and other rivers. Thailand is largely an agricultural society, growing rice, fruit and vegetables and raising animals. The Gulf of Thailand is teeming with fish, the climate is good and most foods grow very easily here. If you stay in the countryside, you quickly become aware that nearly all you need to survive grows around you. In the villages, a strong culture of sharing resources was once common; one household would slaughter an animal and it would be shared among everyone in the village.

Rice farmers in Thailand are the backbone of Thai agriculture and their crop is the lifeblood of Thailand. Glutinous or 'sticky' rice is popular in the north and northeast, but in the rest of the country the long-grain variety is dominant. For many years, rice was the country's main export and it still remains the staple part of the Thai diet, providing strength and energy.

To bulk up the rice and add flavour, a spicy, fairly runny, curry sauce is always served – the effect is to make you eat more rice! Traditionally, rice is eaten three times a day, and curry can be eaten at any, or all, of these meals. As you would expect, the various regions of Thailand have developed their own specialities of curry by using their locally grown herbs and spices. The curries of the country's border regions also often reflect the cuisines of adjacent nations. There is a strong Laotian influence in the northeast, a Burmese influence in the north, Malay and Muslim influences in the south, and so on. But the culinary influence of different countries goes beyond Thailand's immediate neighbours. Sri Lanka, India and Persia have all had their inputs, but now Thai curries have developed their own individual tastes, colours and textures.

My mother's speciality was green beef curry. In a big family like ours, she would cook a large pot of curry to feed us all. My father was always busy working or entertaining, but whenever he ate at home he would ask for green curry. I was the same; just before term ended when I was studying in London, I phoned home to ensure a curry would be ready when I arrived back in Bangkok. One of my brothers even told his future wife that his one requirement was that she learned to cook green curry just like our mother!

SERVINGS AND QUANTITIES

The recipes in this book are for four to six people, and they tell you how to make curries as authentic as you would find in Thailand. When you start making the curries, I hope you will experiment, adjusting the quantities of the ingredients to create a hotter, milder, sweeter or more sour taste – just as cooks do in Thailand – so you develop the flavours that you prefer. The best way to learn about Thai curries is to make a big pot, invite your friends round, have a party and enjoy yourself.

left

Different vegetables are planted in rows with irrigation channels between them. This farming technique is widely used in central Thailand, near the Chao Phraya river. Here they are planting shallots and garlic.

above right

Good quality, long-grain rice. It is always bought in bulk in Thailand!

right

Young papaya trees – these are grown from seed and can grow to about two metres in height. Here they are surrounded by coriander plants.

what is thai cooking?

Originally, Thai people lived a waterborne lifestyle, mainly in the central plains of Thailand, travelling on, and living by the rivers, growing rice and catching fish, which was cooked on a wood-fire grill or barbecue. To accompany the fish, they developed dips and sauces, which were made from locally grown herbs, spices, peppers, cucumbers, aubergines and other vegetables, some of which were grown in the rivers, along with various types of limes and lemongrass. The vegetables were, and still are, often eaten raw. As this diet is somewhat dry, soups developed, such as the well-known *tom yam*, which was originally made with fish. At that time, the Thais shunned eating large animals, and when meat was eaten it was always chopped into small pieces. This is thought to be because of their Buddhist heritage. During the sixteenth century, foreigners started to appear in Thailand, introducing significant new ingredients, such as the chilli. Since that time, the Thais have adopted many foreign foods, including curries from India and Persia, and noodles

from China, but they have always been adapted to suit the Thai way of eating, thereby producing a taste unique to Thailand. Food inevitably becomes individual to the place where it is being prepared and cooked, because the local ingredients always have a taste and texture different to anywhere else. Nowadays, fruit and vegetables that are associated with certain parts of the world can be bought anywhere, and so, sadly, this individuality is gradually being lost. I am glad to say, though, that it still exists in Thailand.

What does curry mean?

The word 'curry' is a derivative of the Tamil word 'kari'. This was used in India to describe a type of dish with a strong flavour and aroma caused by the herbs and spices used in the cooking. They were often used to disguise poor-quality meat, which in the old days could be pretty tough and 'high'. A few Thai curries do resemble the Indian version, in which case the name *kari* is used (see Duck Curry on page 90), but the more usual term in Thailand is *gaeng pet*. This literally means 'thickened spicy liquid'. *Gaeng pet* has a broader application than the English word 'curry' and can be used to describe any savoury dish that has been thickened with a paste.

Curry paste was and still is prepared by pounding the ingredients individually in a mortar. If you walk around some residential areas in Thailand in the morning, you will hear the rhythmic pounding of pestles and mortars all around you. Each housewife produces her own characteristic beat as she grinds out the paste for that day's curry. Today, however, most people buy their curry pastes, either freshly made in the local market or prepacked from a supermarket.

Many of the ingredients in Thai curry pastes are considered healthy and even medicinal (garlic is an obvious example), but their texture or taste can make them difficult or unpleasant to eat alone. Pounding and mixing them together gets round this problem, and when the flavours are skilfully blended, ingredients that might be unpalatable on their own become part of something delicious.

left
Different ready-made curry pastes for sale.

right
An array of red, green, pale green and yellow chillies. Bigger chillies tend to be milder and are often dried to intensify their flavour. Thai cucumbers can be seen on the far right of the picture.

Curry pastes form the basis of almost all Thai dishes – the two exceptions are soups and stir-fries. You might be surprised to find a chapter entitled 'Snacks and One-Dish Meals' in a book about curries, but all these recipes use some kind of curry paste as their foundation, and that includes satay, sweetcorn cakes, and rice and noodle dishes.

The differences between a Thai and an Indian curry

The most obvious difference between Thai and Indian curries is that Thai curries are cooked with herbs and spices that are nearly always fresh, whereas Indian curries use dried ones. And while Indian curries are usually based on ghee or yogurt, Thais typically use coconut milk. The resulting textures are as subtly contrasting as cow's milk and soya milk. Another difference is that Thai curries combine vegetables with meat or fish, while in India the vegetables are often served as separate dishes.

What's special about Thai curries?

Because they are based on fresh ingredients, Thai curries are uniquely light and refreshing. They also have very distinctive colours. These are determined by the colour of their ingredients, mostly the chillies and the curry pastes, hence the famous red, green and yellow varieties.

Where does the heat in Thai curries come from?

The heat in Thai curries comes from chillies, pepper (both white and black), garlic, galangal, coriander and onion. All these ingredients are hot in varying degrees. But while heat is a feature of many of the curries in this book, it should always be balanced by three other key tastes in Thai cuisine: sweet, sour and salty. Sweetness is provided by ingredients such as sugar and Thai basil; sourness by tamarind and lime; and saltiness by fish sauce.

the role of curry in a thai meal

When we discuss what to eat, we first choose a type of curry (red, green, orange, jungle) and the main ingredient (beef, pork, fish, etc.). At home, after we finish dinner, we discuss what we are going to eat the following day. Once we have decided on the curry and its ingredients, we then decide on the accompanying vegetables, taking into account what is in season and so on. These will be cooked in a stir-fry. We may then choose another dish to balance the other flavours. If the curry is pork, for example, the third dish might be fish fried with garlic and chilli. We also select a dessert. Early in the morning, someone will go out to the market and buy all the fresh ingredients for the evening meal. In the afternoon, we prepare the curry and the dessert, which takes about thirty minutes. The remaining dishes are cooked around 7pm and ready on the table for dinner an hour later.

Curry is eaten all day

When I was at school, much like today, there was food for sale in school at lunchtime, or you could take your own lunchbox. I usually had some toast and hot chocolate, or eggs and bacon for breakfast. For lunch, I would eat curry noodles, and in the evening we would have a meal based around a curry.

In many households, particularly in the countryside, they will cook a large pot of curry early in the morning, which will be eaten throughout the day by the whole family. The children will take it to eat at school and the adults will take it out to the fields where they go to work. In the evening, it will form the basis of the evening meal, to be eaten together with a stir-fry and a soup.

When you travel on the motorways of Thailand, as in other countries, there are service stations, generally with a small selection of food outlets. In Thailand, these are normally run by local people. There will be a wide selection of precooked food, several different curries and stir-fried dishes, omelettes and fried eggs. You are given a plate of boiled rice, and then you pick a spoonful or two of different dishes to be placed on top of the rice. You can choose as many as you wish, although any more than three or four toppings and the flavours can become a little confused. This will normally be eaten with a selection of raw vegetables, which, along with the condiments, will be provided for you at the table.

Street food

My family home is in the centre of Bangkok, near Silom Road. When I was young, it was a quiet residential area with pleasant houses and large, leafy gardens. Now it has been redeveloped into high-rise offices and apartments. This has naturally

increased the number of workers and residents who need to be fed. There are now many roadside food stalls selling all manner of food. In this area, the stallholders start work at around 4am, preparing breakfast: rice soup, freshly squeezed fruit juices, fresh fruit, coffee and, of course, curry with steamed rice. Generally, the cooks on the curry stalls will begin by preparing a big pot of one type of curry, then move onto the next. Come lunchtime, they will have a selection of at least ten different curries. The food is served as quickly as any Western fast-food outlet, and small tables are set out on the pavement. Much is sold as takeaways to be eaten later, either at the office or at home for dinner. Lunch is generally over by 2pm when the stalls are cleaned up and packed away. The cooks then go to market to buy fresh meat, vegetables and other ingredients for the following day. Their working day is just as long as that of the office workers they feed.

far left
Smaller ingredients such as pea aubergines are often sold by the bowl rather than by weight.

left
A selection of ready-made, takeaway curries.

composition of a thai curry

Why is the combination of coriander, lemongrass and garlic so Thai?

There are three main reasons why the combination of coriander, lemongrass and garlic is so typical of Thai cooking. The first has to do with convenience. All these ingredients grow quickly and abundantly throughout Thailand and they are available all year round. Most urban households will have them growing in the garden. Lemongrass grows just like regular grass, only with more of a tendency to form clumps. Garlic and coriander are also fast growing, and the latter has the advantage of furnishing the cook with three distinct products: seeds, roots and leaves.

The second reason for the importance of these ingredients in Thai cuisine is their contribution to a healthy diet. Unlike Westerners, Thais do not make a clear distinction between food and medicine, and all three plants are considered medicinal. Coriander is believed to enhance the appetite, improve digestion and clear phlegm. Lemongrass is another appetite stimulant and considered to be good for headaches and fevers. Garlic, meanwhile, is thought to cleanse the blood.

Unsurprisingly, the final reason why garlic, lemongrass and coriander are so central in Thai cooking is all about taste. All three contribute to the perfumed clarity that is so characteristic of Thai dishes, both individually and together. Garlic is used to flavour cooking oils (Thais don't like to use oils with a strong flavour of their own) and to provide an aromatic, but largely hidden, base for savoury dishes. Lemongrass lends a fresh citrus taste with hints of mint and ginger. It cuts through oils and fats, giving zest to dishes that would otherwise be cloying on the palate. Coriander, as mentioned above, yields three distinct ingredients. The fibrous roots are used as a flavourful binding agent in curry pastes. The seeds are ground to produce a spice with an orange aroma, and the leaves provide pungency as well as an attractive garnish.

Any Thai cook will have learned through experience the skill to balance the flavours of garlic, lemongrass and coriander according to their own preference. As a result, the cumulative taste will vary from cook to cook and area to area. There is no such thing as the correct combination, only a personal one, which is developed over a lifetime of cooking with these three key ingredients.

left
Anti-clockwise from bottom: lemongrass, kaffir lime leaves, galangal, mint, kaffir limes, krachai.

right
The whole coriander plant is used and it is sold in big bunches.

above right
Lemongrass grows very easily in Thailand. The white, tender part of the plant is the root; the leaves are chopped off and discarded.

smaller varieties, but should still be handled with caution.

Prik haeng are large sun-dried red chillies similar in size to *prik chee faa*. They are deep maroon/red and need to be soaked, cut into pieces, then allowed to dry again before use.

The final chilli is the *prik yuak*. It is large, pale yellow-green and shaped rather like the sweet bell peppers eaten in the West. If a recipe calls for *prik yuak* and you don't have any available, you can use a white Hungarian paprika chilli or even a regular sweet pepper instead.

Thais believe that if you burn a chilli covered in salt it will remove any 'bad spirits' that may be around you. The Isaan people from northeast Thailand believe that eating very hot chillies will strengthen you, and the hotter you can eat the more 'manly' you are.

left
Prik kee noo chillies for sale by the bag.

below
Holy basil on the left and sweet basil on the right.

right
Selling *kapee* (shrimp paste). The price is per kilo (in Thai baht) and ranges from a cheap version made with offcuts of fish, through to the most expensive one that is made with good-quality shrimp.

What are the other key ingredients in Thai curries?

CHILLIES
These were introduced into Thailand around four hundred years ago by Portuguese traders who imported them from South America. Prior to this, the heat element in Thai food had come from pepper and galangal.

There are several kinds of chilli used in Thailand. Here I will introduce you to five of the most important varieties. The hottest is the *prik kee noo suan*, which translates as 'mouse droppings' (the similarity is in the shape!). *Prik kee noo suan* chillies are green when young and ripen to red. When red, the taste is hotter, but the chillies have no aroma. When green they are milder (although still very hot for Western tastes), but have a noticeable aroma.

The chilli which comes next on the hotness scale is *prik kee noo* (without the *suan*), which is called the birdseye chilli in the West. It is at least 2.5cm long and slightly less hot than the 'mouse dropping', but still pretty fierce.

The third kind of chilli is called *prik chee faa*. It can be either red or green and is about 7.5–10cm in length. *Prik chee faa* are slightly less hot than the

SWEET BASIL AND HOLY BASIL
Several varieties of basil grow in Thailand, but sweet basil and holy basil are the ones familiar in the West because they travel well. Sweet basil is an annual herbaceous plant, the fresh leaves of which are either eaten raw or used as a flavouring in Thai cooking. It is not unlike the basil used in the Mediterranean. Thai or holy Basil has narrower leaves and is sometimes tinged with a reddish-purple colour. It has a stronger taste than sweet basil, which is only released when cooked.

SHRIMP PASTE

Kapee or shrimp paste is a pungent preserve used extensively in Thai cooking. It is made by pounding shrimp with salt and leaving them to decompose. *Kapee* smells fairly unpleasant when it is raw (some Thai farmers use it to keep monkeys off their crops!), but, as soon as you cook it, the overwhelming odour disappears. I often think that the smell has the same effect on an untrained nose as walking into a cheese shop does for a Thai person! *Kapee* is at the heart of many curry pastes, and can be used to flavour boiled rice. Mixed with other ingredients such as garlic, chilli, fish sauce and lemon juice it makes *nam prik,* a hot runny paste that is served with fried fish or as a dip for raw vegetables.

left
Fish drying in the sun.

right
Yellow chillies are more rare than the green and red varieties and are usually found in the south of Thailand. Yellow curry pastes use fresh turmeric for colour and if yellow chillies are available they are added too. See page 155 for a recipe that uses yellow curry paste.

regional differences

What are the regional differences between Thai curries?

In common with most cuisines, Thai food is very local. Most dishes developed in specific regions because the people were using what grew around them there. The cuisine has developed on that basis.

Thailand can be divided into four geographical regions, each of which has its own culinary characteristics. The central plains, in which Bangkok is situated, are the most fertile part of the country and the most typically 'Thai'. Because communications are good and the region is the centre of business and government, the central plains have absorbed cooking practices from all over the country. As a result, all the classic Thai curries are eaten in the area. They tend to lie somewhere in the middle on the hotness scale.

Northern Thailand consists of a series of upland valleys and is ethnically diverse, with hill tribes and a noticeable Burmese influence. The climate is too cool for coconut palms, so coconut oil is not a feature of local curries. The traditional frying medium used to be rendered pork fat, which gave northern food a special silky richness, but nowadays most people use vegetable oil. Curries from this fertile region are typically less hot than in the rest of the country. One possible reason for this is that ingredients were historically so plentiful in the area that there was no need to make very spicy food to make a little go a long way.

The northeast of Thailand is known as Isaan. It consists of a plateau about 300 metres above sea level and was very isolated and forested until the nineteenth century. The northeast has an extreme climate, with a long, dry season followed by frequent floods. The fertility of the soil in the region is not good, which may be why, in contrast to the north, its curries are often extremely hot. Food was often scarce and the spicier it was, the further it would go. Other features of northeastern cuisine include the use of glutinous, rather than long-grain, rice, small dried red chillies and a fondness for fermented fish (*plaa raa*) as a seasoning.

Coconut palms grow all over in southern Thailand, so coconut cream and milk feature strongly in local curries. Fishing is the most important part of the economy and seafood is abundant. This part of the country was the first point of contact with traders from India and Arabia, so many of its curries show their influence, for instance in the use of turmeric. This is also the most Islamic part of Thailand – about a third of the population is Muslim – and there is a sharp distinction between the curries made by Muslims and Buddhists in the region. The former are usually cooked with ghee (clarified butter) or yogurt plus stock, whereas Buddhists use coconut cream. Curries in the south are quite hot and tend to incorporate yellow chillies and fiery birdseye chillies, rather than the long red ones used further north. And the cooking of the far south has a strong Malay influence.

What is the difference between wet and dry curries?

Some Thai curries use quite a lot of liquid, which can be coconut milk, stock or water, and so have a soupy or stew-like consistency. They are, therefore, sometimes called wet curries. The idea is that the sauce will coat and cling to the rice served with them. Dry curries, such as Spicy Pork with Long Beans on page 105 and Hot Dry Beef Curry on page 113, have little or no liquid added after the paste has been fried.

making a thai curry

How do I structure a curry?

Most of the curries in this book are fried. This means that during the first stage, the relevant curry paste is gently fried in oil. This is usually vegetable oil, but some of the recipes call for the paste to be fried in the oily component of coconut cream (examples include the Prawn Curry on page 134 and the Chicken Curry with Sour Bamboo Shoots on page 76). This entails first heating the coconut cream over a low heat until the solids and oil start to separate and will ensure that the paste fries properly. If the coconut cream hasn't separated, it will boil instead, which will not produce the desired taste. In Thailand, coconut cream is usually freshly made, so this is not a problem. The trouble with prepacked coconut cream is that it is often homogenised, which prevents it from separating properly. Try to buy non-homogenised coconut creams and milks. There are various brands available and the labels will give you the necessary information. If a recipe calls for the curry paste to be fried in coconut cream and you only have the homogenised kind, add a little vegetable oil to ensure the paste genuinely fries.

If you are making a fried curry, the second stage is usually to add the main ingredient (meat, fish or vegetables) and fry for a few minutes. The third stage is to add the liquid, which will be coconut milk, stock or water, depending on the recipe. It is important that you follow the correct sequence if you want your curries to taste authentic.

The other kind of curry popular in Thailand, particularly in the north, is boiled rather than fried. This involves dissolving the curry paste in the cooking liquid rather than in oil. A good example is Fish Curry with Kaffir Lime on page 125.

What kind of oil should I use to fry the curry paste?

I recommend that you use peanut or sunflower oils, which have very little taste of their own and therefore do not mask the delicate flavours of the other ingredients. Strong-tasting frying mediums, such as olive oil, should be avoided.

Can you reheat a curry?

When curry is sold as street food in Thailand, cold curry is poured over hot rice, so warming up the curry. In Thai homes, a big pot of curry is cooked in the morning and reheated for lunch and for the evening meal. At other times of the day it can be served with hot rice to warm it up.

What can you do to intensify the flavour of a curry?

Adding lemongrass or lime leaves to the stock used in the cooking of a curry will give it a stronger and more fragrant flavour. Another way to perk up a bland tasting curry is to use *nam pra prik*. To make enough to accompany one curry, combine 1 tablespoon fish sauce, the juice from 1/4 lemon and 1 finely chopped small red chilli in a little bowl. Most homes have *nam pra prik* made up and ready to hand for those who prefer their curries to have a more intense taste.

curry paste ingredients

These ingredients are used for stage 1 of cooking.

CARDAMOM
A warm spice encased in green, black or creamy beige pods – green being the most common. Whole pods are used to flavour rice and meat dishes, particularly in the Muslim-influenced south. The pods themselves should not be eaten.

CHILLIES
See page 16 ('What are the other key ingredients in Thai curries?') for the common types of chillies.

CINNAMON
Available as sticks or ground, cinnamon has a woody aroma with a warm, fragrant flavour. Cinnamon trees are native to Sri Lanka.

CLOVES
This sweet, warming spice is used in both savoury and sweet dishes, but like most dried spices, its use in Thai cooking is largely confined to Muslim dishes in the south.

CORIANDER
This herb, also known as Chinese parsley or cilantro, is widely featured in Thai dishes and as a garnish. Leaves, seeds, stems and the roots are all used. See also page 15 ('Why is the combination of coriander, lemongrass and garlic so Thai?').

GALANGAL
Galangal is a rhizome plant that looks rather like ginger but has pink root tips and a unique, pungent flavour. In the West, ginger is often used to replace it, but the dishes won't taste the same.

GARLIC
Thai garlic cloves are small with thin, papery skin, which we often don't bother to peel away before use, but if you are using Western garlic you should peel it. See also page 15 ('Why is the combination of coriander, lemongrass and garlic so Thai?').

GINGER
The root of this tuber should be peeled, then sliced, finely chopped or shredded. As with most herbs and foods, it tastes better fresh. Fresh ginger is known for its warm, pungent flavour. A native of southeast Asia, it is used in many intriguing spice combinations.

KAFFIR LIME
This knobbly lime is roughly the same size and shape as the common lime, but has little juice. The peel is often used in recipes for curry pastes.

KAFFIR LIME LEAVES
The dark green, glossy leaves of the kaffir lime impart a pungent lemon-lime flavour to dishes. They are available in some supermarkets and oriental stores. They keep well and can be frozen.

KRACHAI (CHINESE KEY)
This annual has aromatic rhizomes and yellow-brown roots, and is used as a flavouring. It also has a medicinal value as an aid to digestion.

LEMONGRASS
Fresh lemongrass is common to many dishes throughout southeast Asia. Its rich lemon flavour combines well with other wet spices. Lemongrass is also available dried but tastes inferior. See also page 15 ('Why is the combination of coriander, lemongrass and garlic so Thai?').

NUTMEG
Another spice used in some recipes from the south of Thailand, nutmeg comes in the form of dark brown or white 'nuts'. These should be kept whole in an airtight container and grated when needed. Ground nutmeg does not keep.

left
Coriander roots.

below
Kaffir limes.

right
Krachai (chinese key).

PEPPERCORNS
The white, green and black peppercorns are berries from the same plant, picked at different stages of maturity. They are used whole and ground.

SHALLOTS
The shallot is a member of the onion family, but it has a sweeter and milder taste. Thai shallots are so sweet that they are sometimes used in desserts! When buying shallots, go for the smaller ones. Larger specimens tend to be too oniony.

SHRIMP PASTE
This is a strongly flavoured paste used to flavour rice and curries. See page 17 ('What are the other key ingredients in Thai curries?').

STAR ANISE
These are star-shaped, liquorice-flavoured pods indigenous to China. Like cardamom, the pods are used whole during cooking and should not be eaten.

TAMARIND
An acidic-tasting tropical fruit which resembles a bean pod. It gives a sharp flavour to curries. Tamarind is sold dried or pulped, and needs to be dissolved in hot water to extract the juice (see page 83).

TURMERIC
Another member of the ginger family, this can occasionally be found fresh in oriental stores, but more frequently in powdered form. When the whole spice is peeled or scraped, a rich golden root is revealed. Turmeric adds a distinctive flavour and rich yellow colour to dishes.

liquid ingredients

These ingredients are the liquid element of Thai curries and are usually added in stage 2 of cooking.

FISH SAUCE (*NAM PLA*)

This is the basic savoury flavouring of Thai cooking, for which there is no substitute. Available bottled in oriental stores, it imparts a very distinctive salty flavour. It is made by pounding small fresh fish and/or shrimp with salt and leaving the mixture to ferment for a year or so. The resulting liquid is then strained and bottled. The best *nam pla* has a light whisky colour and a refreshing taste.

far left
A bamboo basket is placed in the centre of a large container with small fish packed around it (any fish too small to be sold). As the fish ferment, the liquid seeps through the basket into the centre from where it is scooped out to be bottled.

left
Containers full of fermenting fish sauce with empty bottles ready to be filled. The fish sauce may be left for a year to 'cook' in the sun. The first pressing is used for cheaper brands of fish sauce whereas the second pressing will be better quality and therefore more expensive.

above
Fish sauce bottled and packaged for sale.

right
Coconut waiting to be grated and squeezed to make milk or cream.

Darker versions are often heavy and bitter – I tend to avoid them. Darkness in a fish sauce is also a sign that the bottle has been open too long. If your *nam pla* has changed colour significantly, you should replace it. Commercial fish sauces vary quite a lot in taste and saltiness, so experiment until you find a brand you like. You should also adjust the amount you use in a recipe according to its saltiness. Use taste as your guide. As ever, you are aiming to make sure the flavours are balanced.

SOY SAUCE (*SIEW*)

Of the two types of soy sauce, the light version is thin, with a clear, delicate salty flavour and is the one most commonly used in cooking. Dark soy sauce adds colour as well as flavour to a dish. Use Thai, Malay or Vietnamese soy sauce for cooking; the Japanese version is too dark and has the wrong flavour.

BEAN SAUCE (*TOW JIEW*)

Tow jiew is a thickish sauce made from crushed, fermented and salted soya beans mixed with flour and spices. Varieties are made using both black and yellow beans, although the black bean kind is more common. *Tow jiew* is sold in jars or tins. Once opened, it should be kept in the fridge.

STOCK

When a recipe calls for stock, the finished dish will be much better if you make it yourself, rather than using shop-bought varieties. The way I make stocks is extremely simple. For a chicken, beef or pork stock, I place the bones in a large pan with no other ingredients, cover them with water and simmer for about 2 hours, skimming off any impurities as they rise to the surface. For a vegetable stock, I place 1 onion, 2 carrots and 2 celery stalks in a large pan of water, together with some coriander stalks and a few black peppercorns, and simmer them until the liquid has reduced by about a fifth.

COCONUT MILK

For all these recipes, I have assumed you will use tinned coconut milk. If the recipe requires coconut cream, open the tin without shaking it, and separate the thicker white cream from the transparent liquid, scooping it out with a ladle.

Many people think that coconut milk is made from the watery juice inside the coconut. In fact, it is made by grating the white flesh, mixing it with warm water, then pressing it. The milk is used extensively in Thai curries and desserts. Dairy milk and products were completely unknown in Thailand until recently – they are not used in Thai cooking, except in the Muslim dishes of the south. Instead, Thais use coconut milk and coconut cream. Both are marketed worldwide in cartons, tins and blocks, and now in powdered form. If you can find grated coconut (unsweetened, not the desiccated kind), you can also make coconut milk with it, by mixing it with warm water and squeezing it. Making your own milk from the coconut flesh is hard work, but it does give a better flavour. It is worth trying if you want to make a really special curry.

making curry pastes

For the true taste of a Thai curry, curry paste needs to be freshly made, not bought. It is best done by pounding the ingredients using a stone pestle and mortar. In Thailand, a good pestle and mortar will be handed down from mother to daughter over several generations. In the old days, each ingredient was prepared individually before being pounded together to achieve the correct consistency. Dried red chillies, for example, have to be soaked, sliced into small pieces, then pounded with coarse salt to break down the chilli skin and achieve the correct texture. There is no doubt that, prepared this way, you get the freshest taste, and it is an easy matter to alter the balance of flavours by adjusting the quantities of the different ingredients – more chilli, less pepper, etc.

However, preparing the paste in this way is time-consuming and hard work. Until about 60 years ago, it was the only way to prepare curry paste and it would only keep for two days or so. My great aunt used to sell curry pastes in the market. Her husband, a sailor in the Thai navy, was away for months at a time. He knew that it was always a problem to prepare and keep curry paste on board, so he developed a technique to make a paste that could be dried and stored for use at a later date. This he subsequently developed into a business, under the brand name *Tan Jai*. Their first customer was the Thai navy! Later, it became hugely popular with Thai students going abroad to study. Sadly, the brand no longer exists, although this type of product is widely available. In the West, only the best-known curries (green, red, massaman and penang) are found, but these recipes will show you how to make your own.

How to make authentic Thai curry pastes

The preparation of the curry pastes is the same for each curry. The ingredients should be ground using a pestle and mortar. Start with the hardest ingredient then add the other ingredients one at a time. I usually start with the chillies and sea salt – the coarse salt helps to cut through the chilli skin. As you add each ingredient, check the aroma of the paste to see how the new ingredient is balancing with the

previous ones. This will ensure that you don't add too much or too little of any ingredient. You are aiming for a harmonious blend with no one flavour dominating.

Any leftover paste will keep in the fridge for two or three days. The best way to keep it fresh is to wrap it in clingfilm and place it in an airtight container. You can also freeze your curry pastes – they may lose a little flavour but they will still taste better than shop-bought pastes. Wrap in two-tablespoon portions so you can use as needed.

With practice, you can expect to grind a curry paste in about thirty minutes. It is hard work, but it can be a great stress-buster and the results are definitely worth it. The alternative is to use a blender. This will produce inferior pastes, but they will probably still be better than ready-made ones. If you do decide to use a blender, lubricate the ingredients with water rather than oil or you will end up with a gluey ball.

Note: If dried red chillies are required, always prepare them in this way: slice lengthways, remove the seeds, cut into 1cm pieces, soak until soft, then leave to dry before grinding.

For the eight key curry pastes, I have given the amount of garlic and shallot by weight, not quantity, since sizes vary widely. This way, you can reproduce the balance of flavours exactly as I make it, and then adjust as necessary to suit your own taste.

left
Soaking dried chillies.

right
These stone pestle and mortars last for years and are handed down through the generations. It always amazes me that there is still a market for them!

below right
A pestle and mortar maker at Ang Sila, a small fIshing village near Pattaya where stone pestle and mortars have been produced for hundreds of years.

curry paste recipes

Green Curry Paste
GAENG KEOW WAN

Makes roughly 20 tablespoons

100g (roughly 50–60) small fresh green chillies
1 teaspoon sea salt
70g shallots, peeled and finely chopped
80g garlic, peeled and finely chopped
3 tablespoons finely chopped galangal
4 lemongrass stalks, finely chopped
1 tablespoon finely chopped kaffir lime peel
1 teaspoon finely chopped coriander root
2 tablespoons white peppercorns
1 tablespoon coriander seeds, dry-fried
1 tablespoon cumin seeds, dry-fried
1 tablespoon shrimp paste

Red Curry Paste
GAENG PET

Makes roughly 28 tablespoons

10 large dried red chillies
20g shallots, peeled and finely chopped
40g garlic, peeled and finely chopped
2 tablespoons chopped galangal
4 lemongrass stalks, finely chopped
2 teaspoons finely chopped kaffir lime peel
1 tablespoon finely chopped coriander root
1 teaspoon white peppercorns
2 teaspoons coriander seeds
1 teaspoon cumin seeds
1 tablespoon shrimp paste

Massaman Curry Paste
GAENG MASSAMAN

Makes roughly 25 tablespoons

7 large dried red chillies
1 teaspoon sea salt
30g shallots, peeled and finely chopped
40g garlic, peeled and finely chopped
2 tablespoons finely chopped galangal,
   dry-fried until brown
4 lemongrass stalks, finely chopped and
   dry-fried until brown
2 tablespoons finely chopped coriander root
1 tablespoon white peppercorns
1 tablespoon coriander seeds, dry-fried
1 tablespoon cumin seeds, dry-fried
8 whole cardamom pods, dry-fried, husks
   removed and seeds scraped out
1 small nutmeg, dry-fried, break the shell off
   and use the meat inside
$1/2$ teaspoon ground cinnamon
8 cloves, dry-fried
1 tablespoon shrimp paste

Penang Curry Paste
GAENG PENANG

Makes roughly 12 tablespoons

5 large dried red chillies
$1/2$ teaspoon sea salt
20g shallots, peeled and finely chopped
40g garlic, peeled and finely chopped
1 tablespoon finely chopped galangal
2 lemongrass stalks, finely chopped
1 tablespoon finely chopped kaffir lime peel
1 tablespoon finely chopped coriander root
1 teaspoon white peppercorns
2 teaspoons coriander seeds, dry-fried
   until brown
1 teaspoon cumin seeds, dry-fried until brown
2 tablespoons roasted peanuts
1 tablespoon shrimp paste

Jungle Curry Paste
GAENG PA

Makes roughly 12 tablespoons

10 large dried red chillies
1 teaspoon sea salt
20g shallots, peeled and finely chopped
40g garlic, peeled and finely chopped
2 tablespoons finely chopped galangal
4 lemongrass stalks, finely chopped
2 teaspoons coriander seeds
1 tablespoon shrimp paste

Kua Curry Paste
GAENG KUA

Makes roughly 14 tablespoons

10 small dried red chillies
5 large dried red chillies
1 teaspoon sea salt
20g shallots, peeled and finely chopped
50g garlic, peeled and finely chopped
1 tablespoon finely chopped galangal
4 lemongrass stalks, finely chopped
1 tablespoon finely chopped kaffir lime peel
1 tablespoon white peppercorns
1 tablespoon finely chopped fresh turmeric
   (if unavailable use the same quantity of
   ground turmeric)

Home-style Curry Paste
GAENG BHAN

Makes roughly 15 tablespoons

100g (roughly 70–80) small dried red chillies
1/2 teaspoon sea salt
100g garlic, peeled and finely chopped
2 tablespoons finely chopped galangal
4 lemongrass stalks, finely chopped
3 tablespoons finely chopped kaffir lime peel
1 tablespoon shrimp paste

Orange Curry Paste
GAENG SOM

Makes roughly 10 tablespoons

50g (roughly 30–40) small dried red chillies
1/2 teaspoon sea salt
20g shallots, peeled and finely chopped
30g garlic, peeled and finely chopped
2 tablespoons finely chopped fresh turmeric
   (if unavailable use the same quantity of
   ground turmeric)
1 tablespoon shrimp paste

accompaniments

Curry Powder
PONG KARI

Not so much of an accompaniment as a vital ingredient in several recipes in this book. This recipe makes roughly 10 tablespoons and can be stored in an airtight container for up to one year.

Whole herbs and spices
2 teaspoons cloves
5cm piece cinnamon stick
2 teaspoons fennel seeds
4–5 bay leaves

Ground spices
2 tablespoons ground cumin
5 tablespoons ground coriander
2 teaspoons ground turmeric
2 teaspoons paprika

Mix the whole herbs and spices together in a dry wok or frying pan. Stir-fry over a medium heat for 1 minute or until their aroma starts to fill the air. Allow the spices to cool, then grind as finely as possible using a pestle and mortar or spice grinder. Mix in the ground spices and stir well.

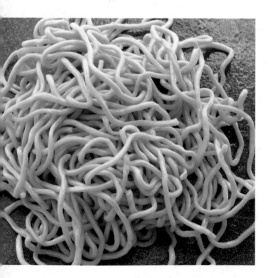

Noodles and Rice

There are no rules as to whether you have noodles or rice with a curry; it is really a matter of personal preference.

Dried noodles usually need to be soaked for about 20 minutes before they can be cooked and drained. They are cooked either by immersing them in boiling water for 2 or 3 seconds or by stir-frying (read the packet instructions for details). The main noodle types are as follows:

THIN RICE NOODLES (*SEN MEE*)
A small wiry-looking noodle made from rice flour. Usually sold dried and labelled rice vermicelli.

LARGE RICE NOODLES (*SEN YAI*)
A broad, flat white noodle made from rice flour. When sold fresh, it is rather sticky and the strands need to be pulled apart before cooking. *Sen yai* is also sold dried.

VERMICELLI NOODLES (*WUN SEN*)
A very thin translucent noodle made from soya bean flour. Only available dried.

EGG NOODLES (*BA MEE*)
The many varieties of egg noodles, from flat, broad ribbons to long, narrow strands, are available both fresh and dried.

RICE (*KHAO*)
Thai rice is long grained and jasmine scented. It is sold abroad as 'Thai fragrant rice'. To make enough for four to six people, first rinse 500g of rice in cold water at least three times until the water runs clear. Then place the rice in a heavy-bottomed saucepan and add 600ml of water. Place the lid on the pan and quickly bring to the boil. Remove the lid and continue boiling, stirring vigorously, until the water level is below the surface of the rice. Finally, turn the heat down as low as possible, replace the lid on the pan and steam for 20 minutes – if the lid doesn't fit tightly, cover the pan with a layer of kitchen foil to ensure a good seal. The alternative is to buy a rice cooker; they are cheap, easy to use and will provide you with perfect rice whenever you need it.

left
Egg noodles (*ba mee*).

right
A vendor brewing and selling fresh coffee. Not so long ago, before so many of Bangkok's canals were built over, this was a very common sight in the city. The vendor would punt his boat along the canals and people would order coffee from their porches on the canal side. Today, this still takes place, but it's mostly in the far suburbs of Bangkok where the extensive network of canals and rivers is still in everyday use.

far right
Hot tea makes a good accompaniment to curry; jasmine tea is the most popular choice.

What to drink with a Thai curry?

Most people will drink water. Others prefer black or white iced coffee or tea made very strong and sweet which rounds off the meal, almost like a dessert. Traditionally, alcohol is only drunk with snacks, particularly with *yam* (a spicy Thai salad, not the starchy African vegetable!). It is not usual to drink alcohol with the main evening meal.

pickles

Ajart should be treated like a side dish. It goes particularly well with dry or rich curries that do not have vegetables included, such as Chicken Massaman Curry (page 80), Massaman Lamb Curry (page 117), Lamb Curry with Rice (page 59) and Curry Coconut Rice (page 60). *Ajart* is also used as a dip for savoury snacks like Sweetcorn Cakes (page 44). This recipe serves 4–6 people. It doesn't keep well as the vegetables go soft; eat on the same day.

Various fruits and vegetables can be pickled, either in salted water or in a mixture of salt, sugar and vinegar. They are used in the cooking method of some of the curry recipes in this book and are also good as accompaniments to the curries – it's largely a matter of personal preference as to which ones you choose to serve!

Fresh Vegetable Pickle
AJART

225ml rice vinegar
4 tablespoons sugar
1 teaspoon salt
1 large red chilli, sliced
1 large green chilli, sliced
450g (total weight) cucumber, shallots, carrots, sliced

Heat the vinegar in a pan. Add the sugar and salt and stir to dissolve. Allow the mixture to cool. Place the sliced vegetables in a bowl and cover with the vinegar. Set aside for 30 minutes, then serve.

Salted Eggs
KAI KEM

8 duck eggs
200g salt
675ml water

Place the eggs in their shells in a preserving jar. Heat the salt and water in a saucepan until the salt has dissolved. Allow the mixture to cool, then pour over the eggs in the jar. Seal the jar and set aside for 3 weeks, after which the eggs can be boiled or fried.

Pickled Garlic
KING DONG

450g garlic, peeled
450ml rice vinegar
200g sugar
2 tablespoons salt

Place the garlic cloves in a bowl, cover with water and soak for 1 hour. Drain and allow to dry for a further hour. Heat the vinegar in a pan, add the sugar and salt and stir to dissolve. Allow the mixture to cool. Place the garlic in a preserving jar, pour the vinegar over the garlic and seal the jar. Set aside for 3–4 weeks. Do not refrigerate until after the jar is opened.

Pickled Ginger
KRATIAM DONG

450g fresh young ginger, peeled and cut into thin slices
450ml rice vinegar
400g sugar
2 tablespoons salt

Place the ginger in a bowl and rinse in water.
Drain and set aside. Heat the vinegar in a pan,
add the sugar and salt and stir to dissolve.
Allow the mixture to cool. Place the ginger
in a preserving jar,
pour the vinegar
over it and seal the
jar. Leave for 3 weeks.
Do not refrigerate
until after the jar
is opened.

SNACKS AND ONE-DISH MEALS

Bangkok People
CHAO KRUNG

The serenity of Buddhist temples is in stark contrast to the overhead Skytrain, the gleaming new underground metro, the water taxis hurtling down the Chao Phraya river and through the canals, and the uncountable numbers of cars, buses and lorries seething around the city in a huge riot of noise and colour. Welcome to the all-day rush hour of Bangkok. As in most Asian cities, people lead a frantic lifestyle, striving to earn a living and spending two or three hours every day travelling to and from work. It is an exhausting day, after which cooking is an effort, one that you can happily leave to others – especially when street food is as good and as cheap as it is here.

Pork Satay with Peanut Curry Sauce
MOO SATAY

Satay was introduced from Malaysia – I remember when I was young the people selling satay on street stalls were never Thai! But satay is now synonymous with Thai food. You can make these with chicken, beef, pork or king prawns. You can also serve thin slices of white bread which can also be dipped into the peanut sauce.

450g lean boneless pork, cut lengthways into strips about 2cm wide
2 tablespoons oil
2 tablespoons palm sugar

for the curry paste marinade
2 teaspoons coriander seeds, dry-fried
2 teaspoons cumin seeds, dry-fried
1 lemongrass stalk, finely sliced
1 tablespoon finely sliced galangal
1 teaspoon chopped kaffir lime peel
1 teaspoon ground turmeric
1 teaspoon salt

for the peanut curry dipping sauce
2 tablespoons peanut oil
1 tablespoon Penang Curry Paste (see page 29)
100ml coconut milk
100ml chicken stock
1 tablespoon sugar
1 teaspoon salt
2 tablespoons lime juice
150g roasted peanuts, crushed

Wooden skewers, soaked in cold water for 30 minutes

First make the marinade. Place the coriander seeds in a mortar and grind to a powder, then add the other ingredients in turn, grinding each one into the mixture to form a paste.

Place the pork, curry paste, oil and palm sugar in a bowl, mix thoroughly, cover and leave to marinate in the fridge for 3–5 hours.

To make the dipping sauce, heat the oil in a pan. Add the curry paste, stir well and cook for few seconds. Stir in the coconut milk, stock, sugar, salt and lime juice and stir to blend. Cook for 2 minutes, stirring constantly. Add the peanuts, stirring, then pour the sauce into a bowl and set aside.

Thread two pieces of marinated pork onto each skewer, then grill or barbecue the satays for about 5 minutes on each side until the meat is cooked through. Serve with the peanut curry dipping sauce.

Spicy Coconut Cakes

TOD MAN MAPRAO

Coconut has many uses in Thai cooking – here it is mixed with curry paste to make a savoury snack.

1 tablespoon Red Curry Paste (see page 28)
200g grated fresh coconut
4 kaffir lime leaves, finely sliced
1/2 teaspoon salt
1 teaspoon sugar
Oil, for deep-frying

Place the curry paste, coconut, lime leaves, salt and sugar in a mortar and pound together to form a paste.

Heat the oil in wok or deep pan. Take 2 tablespoons of the paste and form into patties about 1cm thick. Carefully lower into the hot oil and cook until golden brown. Serve with Fresh Vegetable Pickle (see page 34).

Fried Sweet Potato and Chicken Cakes

TOD MAN GAI

450g sweet potato, peeled, boiled until soft,
  then mashed
225g chicken fillets, very finely chopped
1 tablespoon Massaman Curry Paste
  (see page 29)
1 egg
1 teaspoon salt
1 tablespoon cornflour
3 spring onions, finely chopped
Oil, for deep-frying

for the dipping sauce
3 tablespoons water
4 tablespoons sugar
1 tablespoon palm sugar
2 teaspoons salt
2 tablespoons tamarind water

First make the dipping sauce. Heat the water in a small pan, then add the remaining ingredients and simmer until a thick syrup forms. Set aside.

To make the cakes, place all the ingredients, except the oil, in a bowl and mix well. Wet your hands and form the mixture into patties about 5cm across and 1cm thick. Heat the oil in a wok or pan. Lower in the patties and fry until golden brown. Remove, drain on kitchen paper and serve with the dipping sauce.

Prawn and Coconut Cakes with Plum Sauce
TOD MAN KUNG

Preserved plums have a salty and sour taste. You can buy them in bottles from oriental stores.

275g peeled raw prawns, deveined and finely chopped
90g grated fresh coconut
1 tablespoon Red Curry Paste (see page 28)
3 spring onions, finely sliced
Handful of coriander leaves, finely chopped
1 teaspoon salt
Oil, for deep-frying

for the plum sauce
2 preserved plums
125ml rice vinegar
110g sugar
2 small fresh red chillies, finely chopped

First make the sauce. Use a fork to scrape the plum flesh from the stone. Pour the vinegar into a pan and heat gently. Add the sugar and the plum flesh, stir to dissolve the sugar, then simmer until a thin syrup forms. Pour into a bowl. add the chillies and set aside.

Place the prawns and grated coconut in a food processor and pulse to form a smooth paste. Transfer to a large bowl. Add the curry paste, spring onions, coriander and salt. Knead the mixture, then shape into patties about 5cm across and 1cm thick.

Heat the oil in a wok or deep pan. Carefully lower in the prawn cakes and fry until golden. Remove and drain on kitchen paper. Serve with the plum sauce.

right
Prawn and Coconut Cakes with Plum Sauce

Sweetcorn Cakes
TOD MAN KHAO POD

One of the best vegetarian Thai snacks. Serve with Fresh Vegetable Pickle (see page 34).

Kernels from 4–5 raw corn on the cobs
1 tablespoon Curry Powder (see page 32)
2 tablespoons rice flour
3 tablespoons wheat flour
1 teaspoon salt
Oil, for deep-frying

Mix together all the ingredients, except the oil, in a bowl, stirring well to form a thick mixture.

Heat the oil in a wok or deep pan. Take a tablespoon of the mixture, form it into a small cake, then carefully lower it into the hot oil. Deep-fry until golden brown, then remove from the oil and drain on kitchen paper. Repeat until all the mixture is used up. Leave the cakes to cool, then serve.

Seafood Toast
KANOM PANG TALAY

It's best to use bread that's a little bit dry, maybe a day old; too fresh and it will soak up too much oil. If you only have very fresh bread, put it in a warm oven first to dry slightly.

6 slices of white bread
100g raw prawns, peeled and deveined
100g white fish fillets, any bones and skin
  removed
100g small squid, cut into small pieces
2 eggs
1 tablespoon light soy sauce
1/2 teaspoon salt
1 tablespoon Red Curry Paste (see page 28)
5 tablespoons white sesame seeds
Oil, for deep-frying

Trim the crusts from the bread so that each slice is square. Cut each slice across the diagonals to make four triangles.

Place the prawns, fish and squid into a food processor or blender along with the eggs, soy sauce, salt and curry paste. Blend to a smooth paste and spread evenly on the pieces of bread. Top with sesame seeds.

Heat the oil in a wok or frying pan. Carefully fry the toasts, a few at a time, until golden all over. Drain on kitchen paper and serve hot.

Vegetable Fritters with Curry Paste
PAK CHUP RANG TOD

Any selection of hard vegetables will work well for this snack. Taro (see picture below) is a tuber that should be treated like potato – you can boil, bake or fry it. It is also used in a dessert called *gaeng buad*, where it is combined with coconut and palm sugar to make a sweet soup.

Oil, for deep-frying
50g courgettes, diagonally sliced
50g green papaya, halved lengthways
50g baby sweetcorn
50g carrots, halved lengthways
50g cauliflower florets
50g taro, halved lengthways
50g pumpkin, halved lengthways
50g sweet potato, halved lengthways

for the batter
1/2 tablespoon Home-style Curry Paste
  (see page 31)
110g plain flour
1/2 teaspoon salt
2 eggs
1/2 teaspoon sugar
175ml water

for the dipping sauce
4 tablespoons light soy sauce
1 teaspoon sugar
1 teaspoon finely chopped ginger
1 spring onion, finely sliced

First make the dipping sauce. Place all the ingredients in a bowl and stir well.

To make the batter, place the curry paste, flour and salt in a bowl and mix well. Break the eggs into the bowl, add the sugar and mix thoroughly. Gradually pour in the water, whisking constantly.

Heat the oil in a wok or deep pan. Dip each vegetable into the batter, then carefully lower into the hot oil. Deep-fry until golden brown. Remove from the oil, drain on kitchen paper, arrange on a large dish and serve with the sauce.

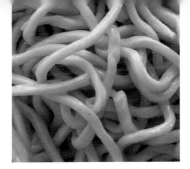

Spicy Beef Balls
NUA TOD

This might look like a kind of burger but trust me, it tastes much more interesting!

left
Spicy Beef Balls

450g minced beef
1 large onion, finely chopped
1 tablespoon Massaman Curry Paste
  (see page 29)
2 eggs, beaten
2 tablespoons fish sauce
1/2 teaspoon salt
1 teaspoon sugar
3 tablespoons unsalted peanuts, chopped
Oil, for deep-frying
Lemon wedges, to serve

Place all the ingredients, except the oil, in a large bowl and mix well until the mixture is smooth. Wet your hands and shape the mixture into golf-size balls. Set aside.

Heat the oil in a wok or deep pan. Prepare a tray lined with kitchen paper to drain the beef balls. Lower the balls, a few at a time, into the hot oil and deep-fry until golden brown. Remove and drain on kitchen paper. Serve hot with lemon wedges.

Noodles with Curry Sauce
GUEYTEOW GAENG JAY

This is a little unusual, as all the ingredients are grilled, giving the dish a smoky flavour.

150g fresh egg noodles
75g beansprouts
75g long beans, chopped into 2.5cm pieces
Coriander leaves, to garnish

for the curry sauce
4 large fresh red chillies
6 large garlic cloves, peeled
2 medium onions, peeled
4 medium tomatoes
2 tablespoons light soy sauce
2 tablespoons lime juice
2 teaspoons sugar
1/2 teaspoon salt

First make the sauce. Wrap the chillies, garlic, onions and tomatoes together in kitchen foil. Place under a medium grill and cook until they begin to soften (about 15–20 minutes). Remove from the foil, then pound in a mortar for about 1 minute to form a paste. Add the soy sauce, lime juice, sugar and salt, stir well, then pour into a serving bowl and set aside.

Blanch the noodles in a large pan of boiling water, drain and pile onto a serving dish. Blanch the beansprouts and long beans in the same water. Arrange the beansprouts and long beans on the noodles. Ladle the curry sauce over the noodles, garnish with coriander and serve.

Stir-fried Beef Noodles with Curry Paste
MEE SUA

Noodles were introduced into Thai cuisine from China some time ago. The Chinese way was to serve them quite plain but they are more spicy now and most definitely Thai!

2 tablespoons oil
4 small garlic cloves, finely chopped
1 tablespoon Red Curry Paste (see page 28)
450g beef fillet steak, thinly sliced
5 nests of egg noodles, soaked in cold water for
    15 minutes and drained
2 tablespoons fish sauce
2 tablespoons light soy sauce
110g beansprouts
2 carrots, cut into fine matchsticks
2 large fresh red chillies, diagonally sliced
2 spring onions, chopped into 2.5cm pieces

Heat the oil in a wok, add the garlic and stir-fry until golden. Add the curry paste and stir well. Add the beef and cook for about 5 minutes, stirring well. Add the remaining ingredients, and cook for a few minutes more. Mix well, then serve.

right
Stir-fried Beef Noodles
with Curry Paste

Curry-flavoured Beef Noodles
GUEYTEOW NUA SAP

Tang chi is made from hard vegetable stalks, mainly cabbage stems, which are preserved in salt.

5 lettuce leaves (any variety)
3 tablespoons oil
225g large rice noodles
1 teaspoon dark soy sauce
2 garlic cloves, finely chopped
110g minced beef
2 tablespoons light soy sauce
1 tablespoon Curry Powder (see page 32)
1 teaspoon cornflour blended with
    8 tablespoons water
1 teaspoon bought *tang chi* (preserved
    vegetable)
1 teaspoon sugar
Coriander leaves, to garnish

Arrange the lettuce leaves on a serving dish. Heat 1 tablespoon of the oil in a wok or frying pan. Add the noodles, stir, then add the dark soy sauce and stir-fry until the noodles are cooked. Tip onto the lettuce and set aside.

Pour the remaining oil into the wok, add the garlic and fry until golden. Add the minced beef, light soy sauce and curry powder and stir well, cooking for about 5 minutes. Stir in the cornflour paste and add the *tang chi* and sugar. Pour over the noodles, garnish with coriander and serve.

Spicy Crispy Noodles
MEE KROP

Mee krop has a sweet taste and is very popular in America; it is always on the menu in Thai restaurants there and is eaten as a dish in its own right, whereas in Thailand it would be served with a curry. Dried shrimp (*gung haeng*) is a dry, salty flavouring that is made by boiling and peeling shrimps and leaving them out in the sun to dry.

Oil, for deep-frying
225g thin rice noodles

for the sauce
2 tablespoons oil
150g firm tofu, cut into 6mm cubes
75g dried shrimp (*gung haeng*)
1 tablespoon Orange Curry Paste
   (see page 31)
3 tablespoons fish sauce
2 tablespoons palm sugar
2 tablespoons tamarind water

for the garnish
2 tablespoons oil
1 egg, lightly beaten
75g beansprouts
3 spring onions, cut into 2.5cm slivers
2 medium fresh red chillies, deseeded and
   finely sliced
20 cloves of Pickled Garlic, finely sliced across
   (see page 34)

Heat the oil in a wok over a medium heat. Add the noodles and deep-fry until golden brown and crisp. Drain and set aside.

To make the sauce, heat the oil in the wok, add the tofu and stir-fry until crisp. Remove and set aside. Stir-fry the dried shrimp until crisp. Remove and set aside. Add the curry paste to the wok, stir well, then add the fish sauce, palm sugar and tamarind water. Continue stirring until the mixture begins to caramelise. Add the reserved tofu and dried shrimp, stir quickly, then remove from the heat.

In another wok, heat the oil for the garnish. Drip in the egg mixture to make little ribbons of cooked egg. Drain and set aside.

Return the sauce to the heat and crumble in the crispy noodles, mixing gently. Transfer to a serving dish, sprinkle with the beansprouts, spring onions, cooked egg, sliced chilli and pickled garlic and serve.

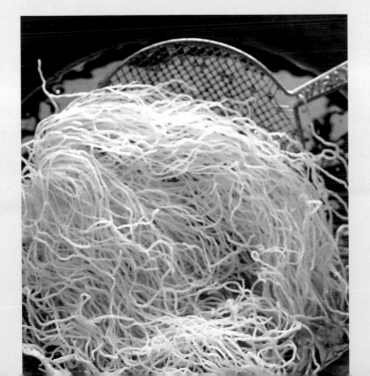

Thai Fried Noodles with Crab
MEE PAD ROO

4 tablespoons oil
1 tablespoon Massaman Curry Paste
   (see page 29)
2 large eggs
225g thin rice noodles, soaked in water for
   30 minutes and drained
4 spring onions, finely sliced
225g fresh white crabmeat, shredded
110g beansprouts
4 tablespoons fish sauce
2 tablespoons sugar
2 tablespoons chopped roasted peanuts
4 tablespoons lime juice
Coriander leaves, to garnish

Heat the oil in a wok or frying pan, then stir in the curry paste. Break the eggs into the wok, cook for 1 minute and stir.

Add the noodles, stir well, then add the remaining ingredients in order, stirring well between each addition. Ladle onto a plate, garnish with coriander and serve.

right
**Thai Fried Noodles
with Crab**

Southern Curry Noodles
GUEYTEOW KAEK

450g boneless pork, cut into 2.5cm cubes
2 tablespoons oil
5 shallots, finely sliced
4 garlic cloves, finely chopped
1 tablespoon Penang Curry Paste (see page 29)
450ml coconut milk
2 tablespoons fish sauce
2 teaspoons sugar
2 tablespoons *chipo* (preserved radish), finely
   chopped
2 tablespoons ground roasted peanuts
225g small rice noodles, soaked in cold water
   for 30 minutes and drained
2 hard-boiled eggs, peeled and quartered
Coriander leaves, to garnish

Place the pork in a small pan and cover with water. Bring to the boil, then simmer gently for 15 minutes. Remove from the heat and set aside.

Heat the oil in a wok and fry the shallots until golden brown and crisp. Remove and set aside. Add the garlic to the wok and stir-fry for a few seconds until golden brown. Stir in the curry paste and cook for a few seconds. Add the coconut milk, stir thoroughly, then add the pork, stirring to ensure each piece is covered with the curry. Add the fish sauce, sugar, *chipo* and ground roasted peanuts. Stir well and cook for about 5 minutes.

Prepare four serving bowls. Bring a saucepan of water to the boil, place the noodles in a strainer with a handle and dip into the water for 2–3 seconds to warm through. Drain and divide between the serving bowls. Arrange the quartered egg on top of the noodles. Ladle the curry over the noodles. Top with the fried shallots and coriander leaves and serve.

Noodles with Chicken, Pork and Prawns
BA MEE SIAM

275g dried egg noodles
3 tablespoons oil
1 medium onion, thinly sliced
2 teaspoons peeled and finely chopped
   fresh ginger
1 tablespoon Red Curry Paste (see page 28)
2 tablespoons fish sauce
150g chicken breast, thinly sliced
150g boneless pork, thinly sliced
150g raw prawns, peeled and deveined
1 tablespoon light soy sauce
175g beansprouts
3 spring onions, cut into 5cm lengths
2 limes, cut into wedges, to garnish

Cook the noodles in boiling water according to the instructions on the packet. Drain and rinse under cold water. Tip them into a bowl and mix with 1 tablespoon of the oil.

Heat the remaining oil in a wok and fry the onion and ginger until soft. Add the curry paste, stirring well, then add the fish sauce, chicken, pork and prawns. Cook for 2–3 minutes, stirring constantly. Add the noodles, light soy sauce, beansprouts and spring onions. Stir-fry for 5–6 minutes. Ladle into a large serving dish and serve hot or cold with the lime wedges.

Vegetarian Fried Rice
KHAO PAD JAY

This is a great way to use up day-old rice as it is best made with rice that is a little dry. .

2 tablespoons oil
1 medium onion, cut into eighths
1 tablespoon Jungle Curry Paste (see page 30)
2 eggs
480g cooked rice
50g peas, fresh or frozen
50g baby sweetcorn, sliced diagonally
4 dried Chinese mushrooms, soaked in hot
**   water for 20 minutes, then drained and**
**   squeezed, stems removed, cap sliced**
2 tablespoons light soy sauce
1 teaspoon sugar
2 spring onions, thinly sliced
2 large fresh red chillies, thinly sliced

Heat the oil in a wok. Add the onion and curry paste and stir-fry briefly. Break in the eggs, stirring well for a few minutes until nearly cooked, then add the rice and the remaining ingredients in turn, stirring between each addition. Turn into a dish and serve.

Lamb Curry with Rice
KHAO MOK KAEK

Fresh Vegetable Pickle (see page 34) is a great contrasting accompaniment to this rich curry, which is just as frequently made with chicken, instead of lamb.

900g lean lamb, cut into cubes
600ml water
4 cardamom pods
10 black or white peppercorns
4 cloves
1 medium onion, sliced
1/2 teaspoon salt
450g rice, washed and drained
2 teaspoons Curry Powder (see page 32)
2 garlic cloves, crushed
5cm stick of cinnamon

Place the lamb and water in a large pan with the cardamom pods, peppercorns, cloves, onion and salt. Bring to the boil, then simmer gently until the meat is cooked (3–4 minutes).

Remove the meat and set aside, reserving the stock (strained if you wish) in the pan.

Add the rice, curry powder, garlic and cinnamon stick to the stock and bring to the boil. Add the meat and stir well. Bring back to the boil, reduce the heat and cover with a lid. Simmer for 15–20 minutes. Remove from the heat and serve.

Curry Coconut Rice
KHAO GAREE KAI

Crispy onions are deep-fried slices of onion which can be bought ready-made or just as easily prepared at home.

2 tablespoons oil
2 garlic cloves, finely chopped
2 tablespoons Home-style Curry Paste
  (see page 31)
450g long-grain rice
1 teaspoon ground turmeric
800ml coconut milk
1 teaspoon salt
5 kaffir lime leaves

for the garnish
3 hard-boiled eggs, peeled and quartered
1 small cucumber, thinly sliced
2 large fresh red chillies, thinly sliced
2 tablespoons crispy fried onions

Heat the oil in a large heavy-based pan. Add the garlic and fry over a low heat until golden brown. Add the curry paste and stir well. Add the rice and turmeric and cook for 2 minutes, stirring well.

Heat the coconut milk in a separate pan until almost boiling. Pour the coconut milk over the rice, stirring constantly, until the mixture comes to the boil. Add the salt and kaffir lime leaves. Cover with a tight-fitting lid, reduce the heat to very low and simmer for 25 minutes.

Remove the lid, stir well and pile the rice onto a platter. Garnish with the eggs, cucumber and chillies and scatter the fried onion on top.

right
Curry Coconut Rice

Fried Curried Rice with Prawns
KHAO PAD PONG KARI KUNG

2 tablespoons oil
1 garlic clove, finely chopped
2 small fresh red chillies, finely chopped
225g raw prawns, peeled and deveined
1 small onion, finely chopped
480g plain cooked rice
2 tablespoons fish sauce
2 tablespoons light soy sauce
1 tablespoon Curry Powder (see page 32)
1 teaspoon sugar
2 spring onions, chopped into 5cm lengths
Coriander leaves, to garnish

Heat the oil in a wok or frying pan. Add the garlic and fry until golden. Stir in the chillies and prawns, cook for a few minutes, then add the onion and cooked rice and stir quickly, cooking for a couple of minutes. Add the remaining ingredients and stir to mix thoroughly. Turn onto a serving dish and garnish with coriander leaves.

Chicken Fried Rice with Green Curry Paste
KHAO PAD KEOW WAN GAI

If I'm cooking at home, this is my favourite dish to make for myself because it's easy and makes a meal in one.

2 tablespoons oil
1 tablespoon Green Curry Paste (see page 28)
1 skinless chicken breast fillet, cut into
  small pieces
2 eggs
450g cooked rice
110g peas, fresh or frozen
2 spring onions, finely chopped
1 tablespoon fish sauce
1 tablespoon light soy sauce

Heat the oil in a wok. Add the curry paste and stir-fry for 1 minute, then add the chicken and stir well, cooking for about 2 minutes. Break in the eggs, stir until nearly cooked, then add the remaining ingredients in turn, stirring between each addition. Serve hot or cold.

Stuffed Curry Mussels
MOK HOY

This is my grandmother's recipe and she used to cook it when we holidayed by the beach in Hua Hin, not far from Bangkok. It looks and tastes wonderful.

left
Stuffed Curry Mussels

900g mussels
225ml coconut cream (see page 25)
1 tablespoon Red Curry Paste (see page 28)
2 eggs
2 tablespoons fish sauce
1 teaspoon sugar
4 kaffir lime leaves, finely chopped
1 large fresh red chilli, thinly sliced lengthways

Discard any open or broken mussels, scrub the shells with a brush and remove any beards. Soak the mussels in a bowl of cold water for 15 minutes and drain. Separate the mussel shells, discarding the halves without the flesh.

Stir together the coconut cream and curry paste in a bowl. Break in the eggs and stir well. Add the fish sauce, sugar and kaffir lime leaves and stir well.

Spread a teaspoonful of stuffing on each mussel and top with sliced red chilli. Place the mussels in a steamer over boiling water for 10 minutes. Remove and serve.

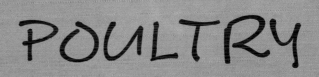
POULTRY

Rice Farmers
CHAO NA

When I was an art student, about ten of us went to stay with a classmate whose parents were rice farmers in Ayutthaya, the former capital of Thailand. We went to paint the landscape. The traditional wooden house was elevated on stilts overlooking the fields of golden green rice, swaying in the fresh clean breeze. Water buffalo were cooling off by wallowing in a nearby pond. Under the house lived chickens and ducks, and there was a small kitchen garden devoted to vegetables and herbs for family meals. Fish came from the small ponds dotted around the rice fields. The self-sufficient economy promoted by

His Majesty King Bhumibol, the present king of Thailand, was very evident here: grow what you need to live on, then sell any surplus.

In the morning, before we were up, my friend's mother would cook us a big pot of wonderful chicken curry, made of course with one of her own free-range chickens. We could take the rice and curry out into the fields for lunch, or go back home and eat. She treated us as her own children and we respected her as we would our own mothers – the Thai way.

Spicy Roast Chicken
GAI OB

Why not try this instead of your usual Sunday roast? The curry paste will give it a Thai twist.

1.3kg whole chicken
3 tablespoons oil
2 tablespoons Kua Curry Paste (see page 30)
2 tablespoons light soy sauce
2 teaspoons brown sugar
1 tablespoon lime juice

Preheat the oven to 180°C/350°F/gas mark 4. Use a large cleaver to split the chicken in half down the backbone. Place the chicken, skin-side up, on a rack in a roasting tin and cook for 30 minutes.

Heat the oil in a pan and add the curry paste, stirring well. Add the soy sauce, sugar and lime juice, stirring constantly until combined.

Brush the sauce over the chicken and bake it for a further 30 minutes, or until cooked through. Serve warm or at room temperature.

Chicken Penang
PENANG GAI

This dish is of Malaysian origin and has always been one of the most popular curries in my restaurants in London and America. Now you can make it yourself at home.

450ml coconut cream (see page 25)
2 tablespoons oil
2 tablespoons Penang Curry Paste (see page 29)
450g boneless chicken breast, thinly sliced
3 tablespoons fish sauce
2 teaspoons sugar
4 kaffir lime leaves, finely chopped
2 large fresh red chillies, thinly sliced
20 holy basil leaves

Gently heat the coconut cream in a small pan, but do not let it boil. Remove and set aside, reserving 1 tablespoon as a garnish.

Heat the oil in a wok or pan, add the curry paste and stir-fry briefly for about 5 minutes. Add the chicken and stir-fry until it is lightly cooked. Stir in the coconut cream, fish sauce and sugar, stir well for a few minutes, then add the lime leaves, chillies and basil. Spoon into a bowl and top with the reserved coconut cream.

right
Chicken Penang

Spicy Coconut Chicken

GAI KRATI

Palm sugar is made from the sap of the coconut palm and has a rich caramel taste. If you can't find it, use soft brown sugar.

2 tablespoons oil
2 tablespoons Kua Curry Paste (see page 30)
450ml coconut cream (see page 25)
2 lemongrass stalks, chopped
2 tablespoons fish sauce
1 tablespoon palm sugar
1/2 teaspoon salt
1.5kg whole chicken, jointed into 8–10 pieces
4 kaffir lime leaves, finely sliced
2 large fresh red chillies, finely sliced

Heat the oil in a large pan, add the curry paste and stir well. Add the coconut cream, lemongrass, fish sauce, sugar and salt and stir the mixture to combine. Add the chicken pieces and stir until well-coated with the sauce. Bring to the boil, then simmer, uncovered, for 30 minutes or until the chicken is tender.

Ladle into a serving dish and garnish with the kaffir lime leaves and red chillies.

Southern Chicken Curry

GAI KELEK

Kelek is the Thai name for a fishing boat. These boats are brightly painted and the curry reflects their colours. In this dish, butter is used as well as oil, a sign of the Malay Muslim influence.

left
**Southern
Chicken Curry**

2 tablespoons oil
2 tablespoons butter
1.5kg whole chicken, quartered, then cut into
   small pieces, on the bone
2 tablespoons Kua Curry Paste (see page 30)
450ml coconut cream (see page 25)
450ml water
1 tablespoon palm sugar
3 tablespoons fish sauce
2 courgettes, thickly sliced
3 tablespoons lime juice
2 large fresh red chillies, finely sliced

Heat the oil and butter in a large saucepan and fry the chicken pieces until just golden brown. Stir in the curry paste, coconut cream, water, sugar and fish sauce. Cover and cook over a low heat for 30 minutes or until the chicken is very tender.

Add the courgettes, lime juice and chillies, cook for a further 5–8 minutes and serve.

Chicken and Lime Curry
GAENG GAI MA-NOW

A refreshing dish that is cooked with whole limes as well as kaffir lime leaves.

2 tablespoons oil
2 tablespoons Orange Curry Paste
  (see page 31)
1.3kg whole chicken, jointed into 8 pieces
225ml coconut cream (see page 25)
2 limes, halved
6 kaffir lime leaves, finely shredded
1 teaspoon salt
1 teaspoon sugar
Coriander leaves, to garnish

Heat the oil in a large pan and add the curry paste. Stir over a low heat, then add the chicken and stir-fry for 3–4 minutes, ensuring that the chicken is coated with the paste.

Add the coconut cream, lime halves, shredded kaffir lime leaves, salt and sugar, then cover and simmer for about 30 minutes or until the chicken is tender. Garnish with the coriander and serve.

right
Chicken and
Lime Curry

Chicken Curry with Green Banana
GAENG GAI KLOI

Like green papayas, green or unripe bananas are treated like vegetables in Thailand, similar to how plantains are used in African cooking.

900ml water
4 green bananas, peeled and cut into large
  chunks
1 teaspoon salt
4 chicken legs (thighs and drumsticks)
2 tablespoons oil
3cm piece of fresh ginger, peeled and
  finely chopped
2 tablespoons Orange Curry Paste (see page 31)
225ml coconut cream (see page 25)
225ml chicken stock
2 tablespoons fish sauce
2 teaspoons sugar
1 teaspoon salt

Put the water in a large pan, bring to the boil, then add the banana and salt and bring to the boil again. Simmer for 3 minutes, then drain and set aside.

Use the heel of a knife to chop off the narrow end of the drumsticks. Chop the thighs in half if large.

Heat the oil in a wok or frying pan. Add the ginger and curry paste and stir well. Add the chicken and cook for 4–5 minutes. Stir in the coconut cream, stock, fish sauce, sugar and salt, then cover and simmer for 20 minutes. Add the banana, simmer for a further 5 minutes and serve.

Black Pepper Chicken Curry
GAENG GAI PRIK THAI DUM

225ml coconut cream (see page 25)
2 tablespoons black peppercorns, crushed
2 tablespoons finely chopped ginger,
    ground to a paste
2 tablespoons finely chopped garlic,
    ground to a paste
1/2 teaspoon salt
2 tablespoons finely chopped fresh coriander
    stems
2 tablespoons lime juice
900g boneless chicken breast, cut into
    1cm cubes

for the curry
3 tablespoons oil
1 large onion, chopped
1 tablespoon Green Curry Paste (see page 28)
1 large tomato, chopped
225ml water
2 tablespoons fish sauce
1 teaspoon sugar

Mix together the coconut cream, peppercorns, ginger, garlic, salt, coriander, lime juice and chicken in a non-metallic bowl. Cover and marinate in the fridge for 1 hour.

To make the curry, heat the oil in a wok, fry the onion for about 3 minutes until golden brown, then stir in the curry paste and chopped tomato. Reduce the heat and simmer for 2 minutes.

Add the marinated chicken mixture, together with the water, fish sauce and sugar. Bring to the boil, stirring, then reduce the heat and simmer for 20 minutes. Serve.

PEPPERCORNS
White peppercorns are picked when young and unripe, and then dried. They have a milder taste than black peppercorns, which are picked when ripe before being dried.

Chicken Curry with Sour Bamboo Shoots
GAENG GAI NORMAI DONG

Here, bamboo shoots counter the sweetness of the palm sugar – see page 152 for more about pickled bamboo shoots.

450ml coconut cream (see page 25)
2 tablespoons Red Curry Paste (see page 28)
1.3–1.8kg whole chicken, jointed into small
**   chunks on the bone**
450ml water
450g pickled bamboo shoots
3 tablespoons fish sauce
2 teaspoons palm sugar
5 kaffir lime leaves
2 large fresh red chillies, finely sliced
20 sweet basil leaves

Gently heat the coconut cream in a large pan, stirring well, and simmer for 1 minute. Add the curry paste, stir, then add the chicken pieces and simmer for 15 minutes.

Add the water, bamboo shoots, fish sauce, sugar and lime leaves. Bring back to the boil, then simmer for about 20 minutes until the chicken is tender. Add the chillies and basil leaves and serve.

right
Chicken Curry with
Sour Bamboo Shoots

Northern Chicken Curry
GAENG GAI CHIANG RAI

This curry is from Chiang Rai in the north of Thailand and its strong gingery flavour is characteristic of Burmese cooking.

2 tablespoons oil
2 large onions, roughly chopped
3 large garlic cloves, roughly chopped
5cm piece of ginger, roughly chopped
2 tablespoons Kua Curry Paste (see page 30)
900g boneless chicken thighs, thinly sliced
1/2 teaspoon salt
450ml coconut milk
2 tablespoons fish sauce
2 teaspoons sugar
2 tablespoons lime juice

Heat the oil in a large pan, add the onion, garlic and ginger and stir-fry for a few minutes. Add the curry paste and stir. Add the chicken and cook over a medium heat, turning until golden brown on all sides.

Add the salt and coconut milk. Bring to the boil, then reduce the heat, and stir in the fish sauce and sugar. Simmer, uncovered, for 10 minutes or until the chicken is tender. Just before serving, stir in the lime juice.

North-Eastern Steamed Chicken Curry in Banana Leaf
HAW NUNG GAI

Every part of the banana tree is used in Asia. Banana leaves are very useful for wrapping food during steaming and they also impart a subtle flavour to the food. If you can't find them, kitchen foil or small bowls can be used as a substitute in this recipe.

450g boneless chicken breasts, cut into small pieces
1 tablespoon Jungle Curry Paste (see page 30)
5 round Thai aubergines, quartered
5 long beans, cut into 4cm lengths
225g dried vermicelli noodles, soaked in cold water for 30 minutes, then drained
3 tablespoons water
4 kaffir lime leaves, finely sliced
2 tablespoons fish sauce
1 teaspoon sugar
5 sprigs of coriander, finely chopped

6 pieces of banana leaf or kitchen foil, each approximately 20cm square
Toothpicks

Place all the ingredients in a bowl and mix well. Take 2 tablespoons of the mixture and place on a piece of banana leaf. Fold the leaf around the mix to form a pyramid, then secure with toothpicks.

Repeat to make six pyramids. Transfer to a steamer and steam for 8 minutes, then serve.

Chicken Massaman Curry
GAENG MASSAMAN GAI

3 tablespoons oil
900g chicken legs
2 tablespoons Massaman Curry Paste
  (see page 29)
450ml coconut cream (see page 25)
450g potatoes, peeled and cut into 2.5cm cubes
4 small onions, peeled and quartered
4 kaffir lime leaves, roughly torn
450ml water
3 tablespoons fish sauce
1 tablespoon palm sugar
2 tablespoons tamarind water
3 tablespoons chopped roasted salted peanuts
2 large fresh red chillies, finely sliced

Heat the oil in a large saucepan and fry the chicken legs until golden. Remove the chicken and set aside. Reduce the heat and stir in the curry paste, then add the coconut cream and simmer for 2 minutes.

Return the chicken to the pan, simmer for about 10 minutes, then add the potatoes and simmer for a further 5 minutes. Add the remaining ingredients, except the chillies, and cook for a final 10 minutes. Add the chillies and serve.

right
Chicken Massaman Curry

Spicy Stuffed Roast Chicken
GAI SOT SAI

1.6kg whole chicken
2 garlic cloves, crushed
1 tablespoon oil
1 tablespoon Red Curry Paste (see page 28)
100ml coconut milk

for the stuffing
1 tablespoon oil
2 medium onions, chopped
225g minced pork
75g unsalted roasted peanuts, roughly chopped
2 teaspoons tamarind water
2 tablespoons chopped fresh coriander leaves
1 tablespoon chopped fresh mint leaves
1/2 teaspoon salt

Preheat the oven to 180°C/350°F/gas mark 4. To make the stuffing, heat the oil in a wok, add the onions and cook over a medium heat for 2–3 minutes. Add the pork and cook for 5 minutes or until the meat is brown.

Remove the wok from the heat, and stir in the peanuts, tamarind water, coriander, mint and salt. Allow the mixture to cool slightly.

Remove any excess fat from the chicken, rub the skin and inside the cavity with the garlic, then stuff with the pork mixture. Secure the opening with a wooden skewer and tie the legs together with string. Lightly brush the outside of the chicken with the oil, then rub with the curry paste. Place the chicken on a rack in a roasting tin and roast for 20 minutes.

Remove the chicken from the oven, baste it with the coconut milk and cook for a further 40 minutes. Remove the skewer and string and serve.

Tamarind Chicken
GAI MAKHAM

Tamarind water adds a sour, zesty taste to curries and other dishes, but you can use lime juice as a substitute – double the quantity though.

4 chicken drumsticks
4 chicken thighs
2 tablespoons tamarind water
1 tablespoon Massaman Curry Paste
(see page 29)
1 teaspoon salt
Oil, for deep-frying
2 spring onions, finely chopped, to garnish

Remove the skin from the chicken pieces. Place the pieces in a large pan and just cover with water. Bring to the boil, then cover the pan and simmer for 10 minutes or until the chicken is cooked through. Drain and cool.

Mix together the tamarind water, curry paste and salt. Thoroughly coat the cooled chicken, transfer to a non-metallic dish, cover and leave to marinate in the fridge for at least 3 hours.

Heat the oil in a frying pan and cook the chicken over a medium heat until golden brown and heated through. Drain the chicken on kitchen paper and serve warm, garnished with spring onions.

HOW TO MAKE TAMARIND WATER
Take a tamarind bundle, put in a bowl and cover with hot water. Leave to soak for about 5 minutes and then use a fork to break up the tamarind, mixing well. Gather up the remaining pulp using your fingers, squeeze well and discard. (Some village people in Thailand dry-fry the remaining seeds and eat with salt and sugar as a snack, but this is probably an acquired taste!). The tamarind water will keep for a few days in the fridge.

Fried Crispy Pheasant
NOK TOD

This is an Eastern-style dish that can also be cooked with chicken. Serve with sticky rice and papaya salad (*som tam*) – heaven!

2 pheasants, jointed into 4 pieces
2 tablespoons Penang Curry Paste (see page 29)
1 teaspoon salt
1 teaspoon sugar
Oil, for deep-frying

Boil the pheasant in a large pan of water for about 10 minutes or until cooked through. Drain and leave to cool. Brush the curry paste over the cooled pieces, transfer to a non-metallic dish, and sprinkle with the salt and sugar. Cover and leave to marinate in the fridge for 30 minutes.

Heat the oil in a heavy-based pan, add the pheasant and cook until golden brown, turning frequently.

right
Fried Crispy Pheasant

Barbecued Spicy Quail
NOK PING

In Thailand this dish is cooked with pigeon but I've used quail here as it is more readily available in the West. Once your neighbours smell this cooking they'll soon be round to join the party!

4 quails
2 tablespoons Penang Curry Paste (see page 29)
4 tablespoons clear honey
1 tablespoon dark soy sauce
1 tablespoon light soy sauce
Lettuce leaves, to garnish

8 bamboo skewers

Remove the backbones from the quails by cutting down either side with a pair of kitchen scissors. Flatten the birds with the palm of your hand and secure each one with 2 bamboo skewers.

To make the marinade, mix the curry paste, honey, dark soy sauce and light soy sauce in a small bowl and combine well. Place the quails in a non-metallic dish, pour over the marinade and leave to marinate in the fridge for at least 3 hours.

Preheat a grill or barbecue to a moderate temperature and cook the quails for about 8–10 minutes on each side. Arrange on the lettuce leaves and serve.

Roast Duck with Lychee Curry
GAENG BET YANG

Lychees are sweet, juicy fruits that contrast wonderfully with the taste and texture of duck.

1.8kg whole duck
5 cardamom pods or bay leaves
5 garlic cloves, roughly chopped
1 tablespoon finely chopped coriander root
1 tablespoon dark soy sauce
1 teaspoon salt
1 teaspoon sugar
1 teaspoon ground white pepper
20 cloves

for the curry
450ml coconut cream (see page 25)
2 tablespoons Red Curry Paste (see page 28)
3 tablespoons fish sauce
1 teaspoon sugar
5 kaffir lime leaves
225ml water
20 fresh lychees, stoned, or tinned ones, drained
10 cherry tomatoes
20 sweet basil leaves

Clean and dry the duck and place the cardamom or bay leaves inside the cavity. Mix together all the remaining ingredients except the cloves. Spread this mixture over the duck and press the cloves into the skin. Transfer the duck to a non-metallic dish, cover and marinate in the fridge for at least 3 hours.

Preheat the oven to 220°C/425°F/gas mark 7. Roast the duck for 20 minutes, then reduce the heat to 180°C/350°F/gas mark 4 and cook for a further 2 hours. Remove from the oven, leave to cool, then shred the meat from the bird.

To make the curry, gently heat the coconut cream in a large pan. Simmer for 2 minutes, then stir in the curry paste, fish sauce, sugar and kaffir lime leaves. Simmer for 2 minutes, then add the duck meat. Bring to the boil, slowly pour in the water, and simmer for 10 minutes.

Add the lychees and tomatoes and simmer for a further 5 minutes. Add the basil leaves and serve.

Hot Duck Curry
GAENG PET BET

This is more like an Indian curry because there are no vegetables in it at all, just a little meat. Serve with Fresh Vegetable Pickle (*Ajart*) – see page 34.

2.75kg whole duck
1.1 litres water
6 kaffir lime leaves
1 teaspoon salt
2 tablespoons oil
2 tablespoons Red Curry Paste (see page 28)
225ml coconut milk
1 tablespoon sugar
2 tablespoons lime juice
Small bunch of coriander, chopped, to garnish

To portion the duck, first remove the legs. Separate the thighs from the drumsticks and chop each thigh and drumstick into 2. Trim away the lower half of the duck carcass with kitchen scissors. Cut the breast piece in half down the middle, then chop each half into 4.

Place the duck meat and bones into a large saucepan and cover with the water. Add the kaffir lime leaves and 1/2 teaspoon of salt, bring to the boil and simmer, uncovered, for 30 minutes or until the meat is tender. Discard the bones, skim off the fat from the stock and set aside.

Heat the oil in a frying pan, add the curry paste and stir well. Add the coconut milk, sugar, remaining salt and lime juice and simmer briefly.

Stir the curry paste mixture into the pan with the duck, bring to the boil and simmer, uncovered, for 20 minutes. Ladle into a serving dish and garnish with coriander.

Crispy Duck with Curry Sauce
BET GROB

You need to prepare this dish in advance to ensure the duck is really crispy.

1.8–2.25kg whole duck
2 teaspoons salt
5 star anise
1 tablespoon Sichuan peppercorns
2 cinnamon sticks
1 teaspoon cloves
4 slices of fresh ginger
5 tablespoons rice wine or dry sherry
Oil, for deep-frying

for the curry sauce
2 tablespoons oil
2 tablespoons Red Curry Paste (see page 28)
450ml coconut cream (see page 25)
350g new potatoes, peeled and cut into
  2.5cm cubes
275g carrots, peeled and cut into 2.5cm cubes
450ml water
2 tablespoons tamarind water
2 teaspoons sugar
2 teaspoons salt
5 kaffir lime leaves, finely chopped

Remove the wing tips from the duck and discard. Use a large cleaver to split the bird in half down the backbone. Rub salt all over both halves. Place the duck in a non-metallic dish with the spices, ginger and rice wine, then cover and leave to marinate in the fridge for 4 hours.

Remove the duck from the marinade, transfer to a steamer and vigorously steam the duck with the marinade for 3 hours, topping up the boiling water as necessary.

Remove the duck and leave to cool for at least 5 hours – the duck must be completely cold and dry or the skin will not be crispy.

To make the curry sauce, heat the oil in a wok, add the curry paste and stir well. Add the coconut cream, potatoes and carrots and stir-fry for about 2 minutes. Add the water, tamarind water, sugar, salt and kaffir lime leaves, and bring to the boil. Cover the wok and cook until the potatoes are soft.

To finish the duck, heat the oil in another wok. Place the duck halves in the oil, skin-side down, and deep-fry for 5–6 minutes or until crisp and brown, turning just once at the very last moment. Remove, drain on kitchen paper and serve with the curry sauce.

Duck Curry
BET KARI

2 tablespoons oil
2 tablespoons butter
5 cardamom seeds
5cm stick of cinnamon
5 cloves
2 tablespoons finely chopped shallot
2 tablespoons finely chopped ginger
3 tablespoons finely chopped garlic
700g boneless duck thighs, cut into 3cm cubes
450ml coconut milk
2 teaspoons salt
2 teaspoons sugar
1 medium potato, peeled and cut into
   2.5cm cubes
2 tablespoons Curry Powder (see page 32)
1 teaspoon ground white pepper
2 medium onions, roughly chopped
1 large fresh red chilli, finely sliced
1 large fresh green chilli, finely sliced
2 tomatoes, quartered
Coriander leaves, to garnish

Heat the oil and the butter in a large pan. Add the cardamom, cinnamon and cloves and cook over a medium heat for about 1 minute.

Add the shallot, ginger and garlic and stir well. Add the duck and fry until golden brown on all sides. Stir in the coconut milk, salt, sugar and potato and cook for 10 minutes, then add the curry powder, pepper and onions. Cover and simmer for 15 minutes.

Add the chillies and tomatoes and cook for a further 5 minutes. Garnish with coriander and serve.

Roasted Duck with Green Curry Paste
BET KEOW WAN

6 duck thighs
2 tablespoons Green Curry Paste (see page 28)
1/2 teaspoon salt
2 teaspoons palm sugar
2 tablespoons fish sauce

Trim off any excess fat from the duck. Cut a few slits in each thigh.

Mix together the curry paste, salt, palm sugar and fish sauce. Place the duck in a shallow non-metallic dish and rub it all over with the mixture. Cover and leave to marinate in the fridge for at least 3 hours.

Preheat the oven to 180°C/350°F/gas mark 4. Roast the duck for 45 minutes. Serve hot or cold.

MEAT

Village Market
CHAO BHAN

Village farmers make a living by growing rice that they sell to factories. The rest of their land is used to grow herbs and vegetables, and usually cows or pigs are kept too. These provide food for the family and any surplus is sold at farmer's markets for extra income. At the market the meat stalls are a riot of colour. Strings of sausages, which may be fresh or fermented, smoked or unsmoked, hang from the rafters along with bags of fried pork rinds and other delicacies. Metal trays display cuts of fresh meat alongside glistening offal, and, in the north, they may be accompanied by a few pigs' heads. In Isaan province, shoppers may come across insects — beetles, larvae, grasshoppers, and even scorpions!

In the past, Thais did not eat a great deal of meat, partly because of the influence of Buddhism and its non-violent teachings, and partly because of scarce resources. The eating of meat was largely reserved for religious festivals and other special occasions. Large animals, such as water buffalo which were considered sacred, were only slaughtered for the pot if they were injured. But today, as a result of greater affluence and improved transport, meat is a much more important part of the diet in Thailand than it used to be. Nevertheless, Thais do not eat a great deal of meat by Western standards and the portions tend to be smaller.

Pork in Red Curry with Pumpkin
GAENG PET MOO FAENGTONG

This is a classic Thai curry that combines meat and vegetables, in this case pumpkin. Any kind of pumpkin or squash will work in this dish.

2 tablespoons oil
2 tablespoons Red Curry Paste (see page 28)
900g boneless pork, cut into thick strips
450ml coconut milk
450ml water
450g pumpkin, peeled and cut into small cubes
6 kaffir lime leaves
3 tablespoons fish sauce
1 teaspoon sugar
2 large fresh green chillies, thinly sliced
10 basil leaves, to garnish

Heat the oil in a wok, add the curry paste and stir. Add the meat and stir-fry until golden brown. Stir in the coconut milk, then add the water and simmer for 15 minutes.

Add the pumpkin, lime leaves, fish sauce and sugar. Reduce the heat and simmer for a further 15 minutes. Add the chillies, stir once, then ladle into a serving dish and garnish with the basil.

Pork Curry with Pickled Garlic
GAENG HUNG LAY

This is a speciality of northern Thailand.

2 tablespoons oil
2 garlic cloves, finely chopped
2 tablespoons Kua Curry Paste (see page 30)
900g boneless pork with a little fat, cut into
  2.5cm cubes
450ml coconut cream (see page 25)
450ml stock or water
5cm piece of fresh ginger, peeled and
  finely chopped
3 tablespoons fish sauce
2 teaspoons sugar
4 whole heads of Pickled Garlic, finely sliced
  (see page 34)

Heat the oil in a wok, add the garlic and fry until golden brown. Add the curry paste and stir well. Add the pork and stir-fry for around 5 minutes or until cooked through.

Pour in the coconut cream and stir until it begins to reduce and thicken, then pour in the stock. Simmer gently for 10 minutes, then stir in the ginger, fish sauce, sugar and pickled garlic. Ladle into a large bowl and serve.

PICKLED GARLIC
You can use bought pickled garlic or make your own as shown on page 34. Garlic can either be pickled in whole heads as seen on the right or separated into individual cloves before pickling.

Pork Penang Curry

MOO PENANG

This is quite a mild and not-too spicy curry and I sometimes eat it for breakfast with bread.

2 tablespoons oil
2 tablespoons Penang Curry Paste (see page 29)
900g boneless pork fillet, cut into thin strips
450ml coconut milk
3 tablespoons fish sauce
2 teaspoons sugar
20 sweet basil leaves
1 large fresh red chilli, thinly sliced, to garnish

Heat the oil in a wok, add the curry paste and stir well. Add the pork and stir-fry for 5–10 minutes until tender and light brown. Add the coconut milk, fish sauce and sugar, and simmer, uncovered, for 2–3 minutes.

Add the basil leaves. Stir briefly and ladle into a serving dish. Garnish with the sliced chilli and serve.

Fried Pork Curry

PAT PET MOO

Bamboo shoots are available in tins from the supermarket (see page 152). Once opened, keep the contents in fresh water in a sealed jar for up to a week in the fridge.

3 tablespoons oil
2 tablespoons Orange Curry Paste (see page 31)
900g boneless pork, cut into 3cm cubes
3 tablespoons fish sauce
2 teaspoons sugar
225ml water
175g bamboo shoots, thinly sliced
1 large fresh red chilli, finely sliced
1 large fresh green chilli, finely sliced
20 holy basil leaves

Heat the oil in a large pan, add the curry paste and stir. Add the pork and stir until the meat is well coated with the curry paste. Add the fish sauce, sugar and water, cover and simmer gently for 45 minutes or until the meat is tender,

Add the bamboo shoots and chillies, stirring well, then add the basil just before serving,

Roast Spicy Pork Chops
GADOOK MOO YANG

I've adapted this dish for Western tastes by keeping the pork chops whole. Traditionally, the meat would be sliced and shared around.

*left
Roast Spicy
Pork Chops*

2 tablespoons oil
2 tablespoons light soy sauce
2 tablespoons Penang Curry Paste (see page 29)
2 tablespoons honey
1/2 teaspoon salt
1.3kg pork chops
2 limes, cut into wedges, to serve

Combine the oil, soy sauce, curry paste, honey and salt in a large bowl. Add the pork chops and stir until the chops are completely coated in the marinade. Cover and leave to marinate in the fridge for at least 3 hours.

Preheat the oven to 180°C/350°F/gas mark 4. Place the chops in an oiled baking dish and cook for 50 minutes. Garnish with the lime wedges and serve.

Pork Red Curry
GAENG DAENG MOO

One of my aunts gave me this recipe. Thai people like to eat at home and there is always something special to try in the homes of friends and family.

2 tablespoons Red Curry Paste (see page 28)
450g pork fillet, sliced into medallions
2 tablespoons tamarind water
2 tablespoons oil
225ml coconut milk
2 tablespoons fish sauce
2 teaspoons sugar
2 large dried red chillies, roughly chopped

Mix together the curry paste, pork and tamarind water and place in a shallow, non-metallic dish. Cover and leave to marinate in the fridge for 1 hour.

Heat the oil in a wok, add the marinated pork and cook over a high heat for 5 minutes, stirring. Add the coconut milk, stir and simmer for 5 minutes. Stir in the fish sauce, sugar and dried red chillies and serve.

Stir-fried Minced Pork with Aubergine and Green Curry Paste
MOO PAD MAKUA

If you cannot find long Thai aubergines, you can substitute the common purple-black variety.

2 tablespoons oil
1 tablespoon Green Curry Paste (see page 28)
225g minced pork
2 long Thai aubergines, thickly sliced
2 tablespoons bean sauce (see page 25)
1 tablespoon light soy sauce
1 teaspoon sugar
20 sweet basil leaves
1 large fresh red chilli, finely sliced

Heat the oil in a wok, add the curry paste and stir well. Stir in the pork, then add the aubergine and stir again, cooking for about 8 minutes. Add the bean sauce, soy sauce and sugar, then stir-fry for about 3 minutes (cover the pan with a lid or foil and the steam will help it cook faster).

Add the basil and chilli, stir thoroughly, then ladle into a dish and serve.

Spicy Pork with Long Beans
MOO PAD PRIK KING

Make sure you cook the beans very briefly – they should be slightly crunchy rather than soft. See page 156 for more on long beans.

left
Spicy Pork with
Long Beans

2 tablespoons oil
1 tablespoon Red Curry Paste (see page 28)
225g boneless pork, finely sliced
225g long beans, chopped into 2.5cm pieces
2 tablespoons fish sauce
1 teaspoon sugar
1 tablespoon ground roasted peanuts
4 kaffir lime leaves, finely chopped

Heat the oil in a wok, add the curry paste and stir well. Add the pork and stir-fry until just cooked, then add the long beans, fish sauce, sugar, peanuts, kaffir lime leaves. Stir-fry until the beans are just cooked, then serve on a platter, with noodles if liked.

Spicy Spare Ribs
KUA HAENG SI KRONG MOO

This is a very quick and easy dish to cook. Use young spare ribs if you can get them.

3 tablespoons oil
900g spare ribs, chopped into 3cm pieces
1 tablespoon Kua Curry Paste (see page 30)
125ml coconut cream (see page 25)
2 tablespoons fish sauce
1 teaspoon palm sugar
5 kaffir lime leaves, finely sliced

Heat the oil in a wok and fry the ribs for 5–10 minutes until cooked through and golden brown on all sides. Add the curry paste, stir, and very slowly add the coconut cream along with the remaining ingredients, stirring gently all the time. Bring to the boil and simmer for a few minutes. Ladle into a dish and serve.

Spare Rib Curry with Bitter Melon
GAENG MARAK

Bitter melon is pear shaped with a green warty skin, and is in fact an immature melon. It is sometimes compared to cucumbers but has the bitterness of chicory leaves. It can be found in most Chinese supermarkets. Use young spare ribs if you can get them because the meat is more tender.

2 tablespoons oil
2 tablespoons Kua Curry Paste (see page 30)
1.3 litres water
2 lemongrass stalks, cut into 5cm lengths
5 kaffir lime leaves
3 tablespoons fish sauce
1 teaspoon salt
2 teaspoons sugar
700g spare ribs, chopped into 3cm pieces
2 bitter melons, halved lengthways, then sliced into wedges about 3cm wide
2 spring onions, roughly chopped
3 coriander sprigs, finely chopped, to garnish

Heat the oil in a wok, add the curry paste and stir well. Add the water, lemongrass, kaffir lime leaves, fish sauce, salt and sugar, then bring to the boil. Add the spare ribs, reduce the heat and simmer for 10–15 minutes.

Add the bitter melon and cook gently for a further 4–5 minutes, then add the spring onions. Garnish with coriander and serve.

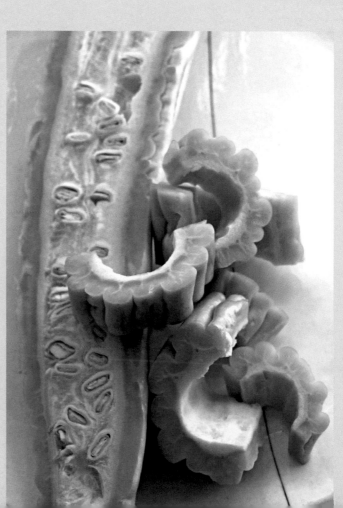

Northern Mixed Meat Curry
GAENG HOH

The idea behind this dish is that it uses up leftovers. Whatever remains from yesterday's dinner – curry, noodles, fried vegetables – all are combined using this method to make a new dish. 'Hoh' is northern dialect for 'throw' – it's all thrown together!

left
Northern Mixed
Meat Curry

3 tablespoons oil
2 tablespoons Red Curry Paste (see page 28)
225g boneless pork, cut into thin strips
225g beef steak, cut into thin strips
125ml water
110g round Thai aubergines, quartered
110g long beans, cut into 3cm pieces
110g bamboo shoots, thinly sliced
3 tablespoons fish sauce
1 teaspoon sugar
225g vermicelli noodles, soaked in cold water
  for 30 minutes, then drained
2 large fresh red chillies, finely sliced
20 sweet basil leaves, to garnish

Heat the oil in a wok, add the curry paste and stir. Add the meat and water, bring to the boil, then simmer for 10 minutes.

Add the remaining ingredients in turn and stir-fry, mixing well, for 3 minutes. Ladle into a dish and serve garnished with the basil leaves.

Wild Boar Curry
GAENG RHAN MOO PA

Wild pig is not unusual in Thailand and more or less any cut can be used. Its meat is more chewy than normal pork and the skin is nice and crunchy. Wild boar will work just as well, but if it is not available, farmed pork can be substituted.

225ml water
450g boneless pork, thinly sliced

for the curry
2 tablespoons oil
2 tablespoons Home-style Curry Paste
  (see page 31)
900ml water
Ground Thai aubergines, quartered
10 long beans, cut into 3cm lengths
150g bamboo shoots
5 kaffir lime leaves
1 tablespoon finely sliced *krachai* (see page 23)
2 large fresh red chillies, finely sliced
20 basil leaves

Bring the water to the boil in a large pan, add the pork and simmer slowly until tender. Remove the meat from the water and set aside.

Heat the oil in a wok, add the curry paste and stir, then add the meat and stir-fry, ensuring it is coated in the paste. Add the remaining ingredients, except the chillies and basil, then stir and simmer for 10 minutes. Add the chillies and basil and serve.

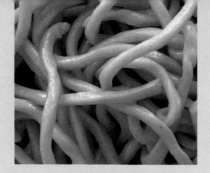

Dry Beef Curry
GAENG NUA YALA

The only liquid in this curry is the small amount of stock so it is known as a dry curry. It's from Yala, in the south of Thailand. Curry doesn't have to be served with rice, it's good with noodles too.

2 tablespoons oil
3 medium onions, sliced
1 tablespoon grated ginger
3 garlic cloves, crushed
1 cinnamon stick
2 tablespoons Massaman Curry Paste
  (see page 29)
900g blade or skirt steak, cut into small chunks
125ml beef stock
1 tablespoon tamarind water
1 teaspoon sugar
1/2 teaspoon salt

Heat the oil in a large pan, add the onions, ginger, garlic and cinnamon and stir over a low heat until the onion is soft.

Add the curry paste and meat, stirring to ensure the meat is well coated. Add the stock, tamarind water, sugar and salt, then cover and cook over a low heat for 1 hour or until the meat is tender. Remove the cinnamon stick before serving. Serve with noodles or rice.

right
Dry Beef Curry

Beef Curry from Pattani
GAENG NUA PATTANI

I first ate this dish many years ago when visiting an aunt in Pattani in the south of Thailand.

3 tablespoons oil
2 tablespoons Massaman Curry Paste
  (see page 29)
900g chuck steak, cut evenly into 3cm cubes
450ml water
450g carrots, cut into 2.5cm chunks
2 medium onions, cut into eighths
2 teaspoons salt
1 teaspoon ground turmeric
1 teaspoon ground white pepper
2 tablespoons tamarind water

Heat the oil in a large pan, add the curry paste and stir well. Add the meat and stir-fry until tender, then pour in the water and simmer over a gentle heat for 20 minutes.

Add the remaining ingredients in turn and cook for a further 15 minutes, then serve.

Grilled Beef Curry with Figs
GAENG MADUA NUA YANG

In Thailand this curry is made with a fruit that looks and tastes similar to a fig but is a bit smaller. I haven't been able to find it in the West so I've adapted this recipe to incorporate figs instead. I always try and reinvent curries using local ingredients.

450ml coconut cream (see page 25)
2 tablespoons Home-style Curry Paste (see page 31)
450g tender beef fillet, grilled, then cut into thick slices
225g fresh figs, quartered
1 tablespoon finely sliced *krachai* **(see page 23)**
3 tablespoons fish sauce
1 teaspoon sugar
6 kaffir lime leaves
450ml water
2 large fresh red chillies, finely sliced

Heat the coconut cream in a large pan, stirring constantly for 2 minutes, then add the curry paste and stir for a further 2 minutes. Add the remaining ingredients, except the chilli, in turn. Bring to the boil and simmer for 3 minutes. Add the chillies, stir again and serve.

Hot Dry Beef Curry
NUA KUA KLINK

This curry is a speciality of southern Thailand and is normally eaten very spicy hot.

2 tablespoons oil
1 large onion, finely sliced
2 tablespoons Kua Curry Paste (see page 30)
1 teaspoon salt
1 teaspoon sugar
900g beef rump steak, cut into 3cm cubes
4 kaffir lime leaves, roughly chopped
4 small fresh red chillies, finely chopped
1 large tomato, finely chopped, to garnish

Heat the oil in a large pan, add the onion and fry until soft. Stir in the curry paste, salt and sugar. Add the beef and stir well over a medium heat to seal and evenly brown the pieces.

Add the kaffir lime leaves and chillies and continue to stir until the oil separates from the sauce. Cover and cook for about 20 minutes. Garnish with chopped tomato and serve.

Lamb and Okra Curry
GAENG KACHIAP KAEK

It's quite unusual to find curries made with okra in Thailand – this one has an Indian influence.

3 tablespoons oil
2 tablespoons Kua Curry Paste (see page 30)
900g lean lamb, cut into 2.5cm cubes
4 tablespoons water
225g okra, washed, trimmed but left whole
2 tablespoons fish sauce
2 teaspoons sugar
Coriander leaves, chopped, to garnish

Heat the oil in a frying pan, add the curry paste and stir well. Add the lamb, stirring to coat. Add the water and stir well. Cover and cook on a low heat for 15–20 minutes until the lamb is tender.

Add the okra, fish sauce and sugar and cook on a high heat for about 3 minutes. Garnish with the coriander and serve.

right
Lamb and Okra Curry

Green Curry with Beef
GAENG KEOW WAN NUA

Everybody in my family loves this curry, and what's more we can all cook it too!

3 tablespoons oil
2 tablespoons Green Curry Paste (see page 28)
900g tender beef steak, finely sliced
450ml coconut cream (see page 25)
450ml vegetable stock or water
2 large fresh red chillies, sliced diagonally into
   thin ovals
3 tablespoons fish sauce
12 round Thai aubergines, quartered
1 tablespoon sugar
40 sweet basil leaves

Heat the oil in a large pan and add the curry paste, stirring well. Add the beef and stir-fry until just cooked. Add the coconut cream and stir constantly as it comes to the boil.

Add the stock, return to the boil, stirring constantly. Add the chillies, fish sauce, aubergines and sugar, and simmer until the aubergines are cooked. Stir in the basil leaves just before serving.

Massaman Lamb Curry
MASSAMAN KAEK

All my Western friends love this one. It's spicy but doesn't have too much chilli. You can eat it with bread, Indian style. The name Massaman comes from the Thai word for Muslim.

left
Massaman
Lamb Curry

450ml coconut cream (see page 25)
2 tablespoons oil
2 tablespoons Massaman Curry Paste
  (see page 29)
900g lamb, cut into 3cm cubes
2 tablespoons tamarind water
2 teaspoons sugar
3 tablespoons fish sauce
450ml stock or water
6 small potatoes, quartered
4 tablespoons whole roasted peanuts
6 small shallots

Gently warm the coconut cream in a small pan until it just starts to separate. Remove from the heat and set aside.

Heat the oil in a wok, add the curry paste and stir well. Add half the warmed coconut cream and cook for 2–3 minutes, stirring all the time. Add the lamb and stir to coat in the curry sauce. Add the tamarind water, sugar, fish sauce and the remainder of the coconut cream, stirring constantly. Add half the stock, simmer gently for 10 minutes, stirring well, then add the remaining stock and simmer for a further 10 minutes, stirring occasionally.

Add the potatoes and simmer for 5 minutes. Add the peanuts and cook for a further 5 minutes, then finally stir in the shallots and cook for another 5 minutes. Ladle into a large dish and serve.

Northern Barbecued Minced Beef Patty
AB ONG NUA

1 tablespoon Kua Curry Paste (see page 30)
450g minced beef
1 egg
1 tablespoon soy sauce
1 tablespoon fish sauce
1 teaspoon sugar
3 kaffir lime leaves, finely sliced
4 stems of coriander, finely chopped

1 banana leaf for wrapping (or use kitchen foil)
Toothpicks

Place all the ingredients in a large bowl and mix well. Wet your hands and form the mixture into a large patty and place in the centre of the banana leaf.

Fold the leaf around the patty and secure with toothpicks. Cook over a hot barbecue for 20 minutes, turning regularly, then serve.

FISH

Fishermen
CHAO PRAMONG

My life now revolves around my restaurants in Miami (Florida) and Ko Samui (Thailand) —
both coastal locations where seafood is fresh and easily available. The southern provinces
of Thailand all have long coastlines where seafood is plentiful, and which contribute
greatly to the local economy and diet.

I recently visited an old school friend, whose family have a deep-sea fishing business
based in Chumphon in the south of Thailand. I went to see the boats when they came
into port, and was curious about how they worked. My friend explained to me that his
boats went out for anything up to six days, depending on how long it took to fill the hold

with fish. Each boat has a crew of around 20, including the cooks. I tried to imagine what it would be like to be out on the ocean for almost a week, with nothing to look at but the sea and the sky — no television, no shops, no distractions at all, only the company of the crew, who all live together in a very small space. The cooks have to plan and organise enough food for a week at a time, because of course they have to take everything with them: rice, vegetables, sauces, spices, meat and chicken. Big pots of curry are the easiest food to prepare and are the main dishes to accompany the rice. Maybe one day I'll become a chef on one of the big cruise ships from Miami to the Bahamas!

Southern Thai Fish Curry
GAENG PET PLA

2 tablespoons oil
2 tablespoons Red Curry Paste (see page 28)
450ml coconut milk
450ml fish or vegetable stock, or water
1/2 teaspoon ground turmeric
3 tablespoons fish sauce
1 tablespoon sugar
1 tablespoon tamarind water
450g monkfish, hoki or red snapper fillet, cut
** into large chunks**
3 tomatoes, quartered
1 red pepper, cored, deseeded and chopped
1 green pepper, cored, deseeded and chopped
Few coriander leaves, to garnish

Heat the oil in a large wok, add the curry paste and stir well. Stir in the coconut milk, stock or water, turmeric, fish sauce, sugar and tamarind water, and simmer for 5 minutes.

Add the fish and simmer for 6–8 minutes. Stir in the tomatoes and peppers, simmer over a low heat for about 10 minutes until thickened. Ladle into a serving bowl and garnish with coriander.

right
Southern Thai
Fish Curry

Grilled Curried Fish
PLA YANG PRIK GAENG

In this recipe the curry paste is used as a marinade. If you come to my restaurant, Cinnamon Kitchen in Ko Samui, be sure to order this dish!

2 tablespoons oil, plus extra for brushing
1 tablespoon Kua Curry Paste (see page 30)
1 tablespoon fish sauce
1 tablespoon light soy sauce
1 teaspoon sugar
2 tablespoons water
2 trout or red snapper, weighing about
** 275g each, cleaned and trimmed**
Banana leaf (or tin foil)

for the garnish
Tomato slices
Onion rings
Cucumber slices
Lemon or lime slices
Coriander sprigs

Heat the oil in a pan, add the curry paste and stir well. Add the fish sauce, soy sauce, sugar and water, and cook for 2 minutes, stirring well. Set aside.

Use the point of a sharp knife to make 3 deep cuts along each side of the fish. Spread the marinade over the fish, working it into the cuts. Place in a shallow, non-metallic dish, cover and leave to marinate in the fridge for 3 hours.

Preheat the grill. Brush the grill rack with oil. Place the fish on the banana leaf or tin foil and sprinkle a little oil over. Wrap well and grill for about 7 minutes on each side. Serve garnished with the salad, lemon slices and coriander.

Haddock with Green Curry Sauce
KEOW WAN PLA

left
**Haddock with Green
Curry Sauce**

450ml coconut cream (see page 25)
1 teaspoon salt
2 tablespoons Green Curry Paste (see page 28)
1 tablespoon palm sugar
4 haddock fillets, each weighing about 150g
10 kaffir lime leaves, finely sliced
2 large fresh red chillies, sliced into thin ovals

Gently heat the coconut cream in a large frying pan, add the salt and stir in the green curry paste, mixing well. Add the palm sugar, stirring constantly. Add the haddock and kaffir lime leaves, then bring slowly to simmering point.

Reduce the heat, cover and poach the fish for 10–15 minutes, depending on its thickness. Transfer the fish to warmed plates, garnish with chillies and serve.

Fish Curry with Kaffir Lime
GAENG PLA MAKRUT

For this recipe you will not need all the curry paste you make – there will be enough left over to make three or four more curries.

450ml coconut milk
2 tablespoons curry paste (see below)
1 teaspoon salt
1 tablespoon palm sugar
900g firm white fish fillets, cut into 3cm chunks
6 kaffir lime leaves, roughly torn
2 large fresh red chillies, diagonally sliced

for the curry paste
5 dried and 5 fresh red chillies
1/2 teaspoon salt
1 tablespoon black peppercorns
2 tablespoons finely chopped galangal
4 tablespoons finely chopped lemongrass
2 teaspoons grated kaffir lime peel
2 teaspoons finely chopped fresh turmeric (if
   unavailable, use the same quantity of ground)
1 teaspoon shrimp paste

To make the paste, pound each of the ingredients in a mortar in turn, adding them one by one until a paste is formed.

Gently warm the coconut milk in a pan, then add the curry paste, salt and sugar. Bring to the boil, add the fish and kaffir lime leaves, bring back to the boil and simmer for about 3 minutes, stirring gently. Add the chillies and serve.

Mackerel in Red Curry
CHU CHEE PLA

Mackerel is a popular fish in Thailand and this is a simple and satisfying curry.

4 tablespoons oil
3 mackerel fillets, cleaned
1 tablespoon Red Curry Paste (see page 28)
225ml coconut cream (see page 25)
2 tablespoons fish sauce
1 teaspoon sugar
5 kaffir lime leaves, finely sliced
2 large fresh red chillies, thinly sliced
20 sweet basil leaves

Heat 2 tablespoons of oil in a large, deep-sided frying pan, add the mackerel and fry over a medium heat for 5–7 minutes or until the fish is cooked. Remove the fish from the oil, drain on kitchen paper and set aside.

Heat the remaining oil in the frying pan, add the curry paste and stir well, then add the coconut cream and the remaining ingredients. Add the fish to the pan and cook for a further 2–3 minutes, stirring constantly. Ladle into a dish, add the basil leaves and serve.

right
**Mackerel in
Red Curry**

Barbecued Curried Squid
PLA MUK KORLEH

This is a mild dish, suitable for those who are not keen on hot food! It's the perfect streetfood to eat on the beach with a beer. The sellers have portable charcoal barbecues to cook the squid on.

450ml coconut milk
2 tablespoons Curry Powder (see page 32)
1 teaspoon salt
1 teaspoon sugar
1 teaspoon ground white pepper
2 tablespoons tamarind water
900g large squid, cleaned

Heat the coconut milk, curry powder, salt, sugar, white pepper and tamarind water in a large pan, stirring to mix well. When the sugar has dissolved, remove from the heat and add the squid. Leave to marinate for at least 1 hour in the fridge.

Remove the squid from the marinade and place on a preheated barbecue. Cook for 5 minutes on each side, brushing with the marinade. Cut into small pieces to serve.

Fish Curry with Papaya
PLA GAENG SOM

The best papayas to use for this curry are green, unripe ones that are just starting to turn yellow.

left
**Fish Curry
with Papaya**

1.1 litres water
2 tablespoons Orange Curry Paste (see page 31)
450g monkfish fillet, cut into large chunks
**1 small unripe papaya, peeled, deseeded and
   roughly sliced**
1 teaspoon salt
2 tablespoons fish sauce
1 tablespoon palm sugar
3 tablespoons tamarind water
**Coriander leaves and slices of red chilli,
   to garnish**

Bring the water to the boil in a large pan, add the curry paste and stir well. Add the fish and cook gently for about 5 minutes.

Add the remaining ingredients, stir well and gently cook for a further 5 minutes. Serve hot, garnished with coriander and red chilli.

Sea Bass with Curry Sauce
PLA LAD PRIK

One of my favourites, so good I never want to share it!

1kg sea bass, cleaned and scaled
1 teaspoon salt
2 tablespoons plain flour
Oil, for deep-frying

for the curry sauce
2 tablespoons oil
**2 tablespoons Home-style Curry Paste
   (see page 31)**
2 tablespoons fish sauce
2 tablespoons water
1 tablespoon light soy sauce
1 large fresh red chilli, thinly sliced
1 large fresh green chilli, thinly sliced
2 teaspoons sugar
Coriander leaves, to garnish

Use the point of a sharp knife to score both sides of the fish, making diagonal cuts to the bone at intervals of about 2.5cm. Rub the whole fish with salt, inside and outside, then coat it from head to tail with flour.

Heat the oil in a wok. Deep-fry the fish in the hot oil for about 4–5 minutes on each side, or until golden brown. Remove the fish, drain on kitchen paper, then place on a warmed platter.

To make the sauce, heat the oil in a pan, add the curry paste and stir. Add the fish sauce, water, soy sauce, chillies and sugar, stirring well until the sauce is smooth and thickened. Pour the curry sauce over the fish and garnish with fresh coriander.

Curried Fish Balls with Bamboo Shoots
GAENG PA LUKCHIN PLA

Fish balls are like small round dumplings and are made from fish and flour. They can be bought ready prepared in Chinese stores.

2 tablespoons oil
2 tablespoons Jungle Curry Paste (see page 30)
450g fish balls
675ml water
3 tablespoons fish sauce
6 kaffir lime leaves
150g bamboo shoots
1 tablespoon finely sliced _krachai_ (see page 23)
20 sweet basil leaves

Heat the oil in a large pan, add the curry paste, then add the fish balls quickly and stir-fry for 2 minutes. Add the remaining ingredients in turn, stirring well, then bring to the boil. Ladle into a dish, add the basil leaves and serve.

MAKING FISH BALLS
The skin is removed from the fish and the flesh cut into small pieces. It is then pounded, mixed with a little flour and moulded into fish balls. The fish skin is not discarded – it is sun dried or deep fried to crispen and added to curry or noodle soup, or served as a side dish with chilli dip (_nam prik_).

Stir-fried Spicy Seafood
PAD PET TALAY

Being Thai, naturally I think this is the best way in the world to cook seafood!

left
Stir-fried
Spicy Seafood

3 tablespoons oil
2 medium onions, sliced
1 tablespoon Red Curry Paste (see page 28)
450g raw prawns, peeled and deveined, tails on
175g squid, cut into 6cm squares, and scored in
 a criss-cross fashion with a small knife
225g mussels, cleaned and debearded (discard
 any with open or broken shells)
1 large tomato, finely chopped
20 basil leaves
2 tablespoons fish sauce
1 teaspoon sugar
10 sweet basil leaves, to garnish

Heat the oil in a wok, add the onions and cook until soft. Add the curry paste and stir well. Add the seafood and cook over a high heat for 3–5 minutes.

Stir in the tomato, basil, fish sauce and sugar, and stir-fry for a further 3 minutes. Ladle into a serving dish, garnish with the basil leaves and serve.

Stir-fried Prawn Curry
PAD PET KUNG

Prawns are one of the best kinds of seafood to cook very quickly and they go with all kinds of sauce and dressings.

2 tablespoons oil
1 medium onion, finely sliced
1 tablespoon Home-style Curry Paste
 (see page 31)
1 tablespoon tamarind water
1 tablespoon sugar
450g raw king prawns, peeled and deveined
2 tablespoons fish sauce
3–4 tablespoons water
20 sweet basil leaves

Heat the oil in a frying pan and fry the onion until golden brown. Add the curry paste, tamarind water and sugar and stir well.

Add the prawns, fish sauce and water and stir-fry until the prawns turn a bright orange colour. Add the basil and stir-fry on a high heat for a few minutes, then serve.

Steamed Prawn Curry in Banana Leaf
HAW MOK KUNG

For this recipe, the traditional way to cook and present the curry is in a banana leaf cup. To make each cup, cut two 15cm circles from a banana leaf, place one on top of the other and fold round into a cup with 4cm-high sides. Secure the corners with a staple or a wooden toothpick. You need to make 4 cups for this amount of curry.

400g raw prawns, peeled, deveined and finely chopped
1 tablespoon Red Curry Paste (see page 28)
225ml coconut cream (see page 25)
1 teaspoon salt
1 teaspoon sugar
1 tablespoon ground roasted peanuts
40 sweet basil leaves
1 large fresh red chilli, finely sliced

2 large banana leaves
Toothpicks

Place the prawns, curry paste, coconut cream, salt, sugar and peanuts in a bowl and mix well. Cover and set aside in the fridge for 1 hour.

Place 10 basil leaves in the base of each cup. Fill each one with the cold mixture and transfer the cups to a steamer set over boiling water. Steam for 10 minutes. Remove from the steamer, garnish with chilli and serve.

right
Steamed Prawn Curry in Banana Leaf

Prawn Curry
PENANG KUNG

Another dish that is very popular in my restaurant in Miami. It used to be a special but people kept asking for it so now it's on the menu every day!

450ml coconut cream (see page 25)
1 tablespoon Penang Curry Paste (see page 29)
225g mangetout, cut into 5cm pieces
2 tablespoons fish sauce
1 tablespoon palm sugar
450g raw prawns, peeled and deveined, tails on
5 kaffir lime leaves, finely sliced
1 large fresh red chilli, finely sliced

Gently heat the coconut cream in a wok, add the curry paste and stir well. Add the mangetout, fish sauce and palm sugar and stir again.

Add the prawns and simmer for 5 minutes. Stir in the kaffir lime leaves. Spoon into a serving dish, garnish with the chilli and serve.

Spicy Prawns with Peppercorns
PAD CHA KUNG

This is on my new menu in Ko Samui. Peppercorns are one of the ingredients I grow in my kitchen garden there. Fresh peppercorns are more expensive in the West, where you won't find this kind of dish on the menu so often.

left
Spicy Prawns with
Peppercorns

3 tablespoons oil
1 tablespoon Kua Curry Paste (see page 30)
900g raw king prawns, peeled and deveined
3 tablespoons fish sauce
1 teaspoon sugar
1 tablespoon finely sliced *krachai* (see page 23)
50g fresh green peppercorns

Heat the oil in a wok, add the curry paste, stir well, then add the remaining ingredients in turn, stirring quickly. Cook over a high heat for 2 minutes, then ladle into a dish and serve.

Squid Curry
KARI PLA MUK

If you can find it, fresh squid cooks more quickly and has a less rubbery texture.

2 tablespoons oil
3 tablespoons finely sliced shallots
2 tablespoons finely sliced garlic
2 tablespoons Curry Powder (see page 32)
900g small squid, cleaned and thinly sliced
225ml coconut cream (see page 25)
5 courgettes, halved lengthways
2 teaspoons salt
2 tablespoons tamarind water
2 teaspoons sugar
225ml water
2 tomatoes, quartered
1 tablespoon chopped fresh coriander,
   to garnish

Heat the oil in a wok, add the shallots and garlic and cook until crispy and golden brown. Remove and set aside. Add the curry powder, stir well, then add the squid and stir-fry for 1 minute.

Reduce the heat and stir in the coconut cream, then add the courgettes, salt, tamarind water, sugar and water. Cook, stirring constantly, for 2 minutes. Add the tomatoes, leave to heat through briefly, then garnish with the crispy shallots and garlic, sprinkle with chopped coriander and serve.

Pineapple Curry with Mussels
GAENG KUA HOY

How lucky we are in Thailand to have a ready supply of seafood as well as fruit and vegetables. I love this combination of mussels and pineapple.

900g fresh mussels
450ml coconut cream (see page 25)
2 tablespoons Orange Curry Paste (see page 31)
225ml water
2 tablespoons fish sauce
1 tablespoon palm sugar
1 tablespoon tamarind water
400g prepared pineapple, cut into small cubes
20 sweet basil leaves

Discard any open or broken mussels, scrub the shells with a brush and remove any beards. Soak the mussels in cold water for 15 minutes, then drain.

Heat the coconut cream in a large pan, add the curry paste and stir over a medium heat for 2 minutes. Slowly add the water, bring to the boil, then stir in the fish sauce, palm sugar and tamarind water. Add the mussels and pineapple and simmer for about 2 minutes. Add the basil and mix well before serving.

Spicy Squid
PAD PET PLA MUK

Serve with rice and wedges of lime to make a main course.

left
Spicy Squid

**700g squid, cut into large pieces and scored in a
    criss-cross fashion with the tip of a knife**
2 tablespoons lime juice
2 tablespoons oil
1 tablespoon Red Curry Paste (see page 28)
2 tablespoons fish sauce
2 teaspoons sugar
1 medium onion, finely sliced
2 large fresh red chillies, finely sliced
20 sweet basil leaves

Place the squid in a bowl with the lime juice. Cover and leave to marinate for 1 hour in the fridge. Heat the oil in a wok, add the curry paste and stir well. Add the squid and cook over a moderate heat for 2 minutes, then add the fish sauce, sugar, onion, chillies and basil. Stir well for 2 minutes, add the basil leaves and serve.

Squid Curry with Salted Eggs
KARI PLA MUK KAI KEM

I got this recipe from a restaurant in Surat Thani. Usually salted eggs are boiled or fried before use, but here they are marinaded and quickly stir fried, making this quite an unusual dish.

450g squid, cleaned and cut into 5cm pieces
2 Salted Eggs (see page 34)
1 teaspoon ground turmeric
3 tablespoons oil
2 tablespoons Curry Powder (see page 32)
1 tablespoon tamarind water
1 teaspoon sugar
4 tablespoons water
4 spring onions, chopped into 3cm lengths
5 small tomatoes, quartered
10 coriander stems, roughly chopped
3 tablespoons crispy sliced shallots
2 tablespoons crispy sliced garlic

Place the squid, eggs and turmeric in a non-metallic bowl, mix together and leave to marinate for 30 minutes in the fridge.

Heat the oil in a wok, stir in the curry powder and marinated squid and eggs, and cook for 1 minute. Add the remaining ingredients in turn, stirring constantly. The crispy shallots and garlic should be added at the last minute, just before serving.

Crab with Curry Powder
ROO PAD PONG KARI

900g fresh whole crab (uncooked)
2 tablespoons oil
3 garlic cloves, crushed
2 tablespoons Curry Powder (see page 32)
2 eggs
4 whole spring onions, cut into 5cm pieces
1 tablespoon finely chopped ginger
2 tablespoons fish sauce
1 tablespoon light soy sauce
1 teaspoon sugar
2 large fresh red chillies, thinly sliced
Coriander leaves, to garnish

Scrub the crab well. Pull back the apron from the underbelly and snap off. Twist off the legs and claws. Pull the body apart and remove the feathery gills and internal organs. Use a cleaver to chop the body into 4 pieces. Crack the claws with a good hit using the back of the cleaver.

Heat the oil in a wok, add the garlic and fry until golden brown. Add the curry powder and eggs, stir well, then add the crab and stir-fry for 2–3 minutes. Add the spring onions, ginger, fish sauce, soy sauce, sugar and chillies and cook for 4–5 minutes. Garnish with coriander and serve.

right
Crab with
Curry Powder

Chilli Crab
ROO PAD PET

This dish is a bit tricky to prepare, and like all crab dishes, difficult to eat, but it's worth the effort!

2 x 500g fresh whole crabs
   (uncooked)
75g plain flour
4 tablespoons oil
1 medium onion, finely chopped
2 tablespoons Penang Curry Paste (see page 29)
225ml water
2 tablespoons fish sauce
2 teaspoons sugar
2 tablespoons lime Juice
4 kaffir lime leaves, finely sliced

Scrub the crabs well. Use a cleaver to chop the crabs in half, then rinse well under cold water, carefully removing the feathery gills and internal organs. Crack the legs and large front claws with a good hit using the back of the cleaver.

Lightly and carefully coat the shells with a little flour. Heat 2 tablespoons of the oil in a large wok and cook the crab, one half at a time, carefully turning the crab in the hot oil until the shell just turns red. Repeat with the remaining crab halves. Remove and drain on kitchen paper.

Heat the remaining oil in the wok and add the onion and curry paste, stirring well over a medium heat. Add the water, fish sauce and sugar and bring to the boil. Return the crab to the wok and simmer for 8–10 minutes. Add the lime juice and lime leaves just before serving.

VEGETABLES AND FRUIT

Vegetables and Fruit
CHAO SUAN

Originally, Thai cooking contained very little meat and was based on fruit and vegetables.
Different parts of Thailand are well known for different fruit and vegetables; Chiang Mai
and the north for lettuce and root vegetables like carrots and potatoes, and Chantaburi
and the southeast for fruits such as rambutan, mangostan, durian, custard apples and
rose apples. The central plains mainly grow rice, herbs and spices, though they are also
known for fruits such as mango, pomelo and papaya. Ko Samui, where I am now based,
is famous for coconuts. The island was very thinly populated until the arrival of Malay

and Chinese fishing families several hundred years ago, some of whom were Muslims who brought their influences into the cuisine. The main industry on the island centred on growing coconuts and shipping them to the mainland to be processed into coconut milk.

Vegetables vary greatly according to the area of the country they are grown in. For example pineapples tend to be small and dry in the north, big and juicy in Chantaburi, and small and sweet in the south, which is why many restaurants in the south import their pineapples from Chantaburi.

Sweet Potato and Mushroom Curry
GAENG MAN GAP HET

The sweet richness of this red tuber complements the hot and sour flavours of southeast Asia.

450ml water
2 tablespoons Jungle Curry Paste (see page 30)
450g sweet potato, peeled and cut into
  2.5cm cubes
110g oyster mushrooms, washed and separated
6 kaffir lime leaves, roughly torn
2 tablespoons light soy sauce
1 teaspoon sugar

Bring the water to the boil in a pan, add the curry paste and stir well. Add the potato, reduce the heat and simmer for 10 minutes.

Add the remaining ingredients, cook for a further 3 minutes and serve.

right
**Sweet Potato and
Mushroom Curry**

Coconut and Vegetable Curry
GAENG PET JAY

Everyone enjoys this dish, not just vegetarians. To make this an interesting dish, it is important to include a mixture of vegetables with different tastes and textures.

2 tablespoons oil
1 medium onion, roughly chopped
2 tablespoons Massaman Curry Paste
  (see page 29)
450ml coconut cream (see page 25)
1 teaspoon salt
2 teaspoons sugar
450g mixed vegetables (potato, carrot,
  pumpkin), peeled and cut into 2.5cm cubes
450ml water
110g green beans, cut into 2.5cm lengths
110g courgettes, cut into 2.5cm cubes
2 tablespoons lime juice
2 large fresh green chillies, finely sliced

Heat the oil in a large pan, add the onion and curry paste and stir well. Add the coconut cream, salt and sugar, bring to the boil, then reduce the heat and simmer for 3 minutes.

Add the potato, carrot and pumpkin, then cover the pan and cook for 7 minutes, then add the water and bring to the boil, stirring occasionally.

Add the beans and courgettes and cook for a further 5 minutes. Stir in the lime juice and chilli and serve immediately.

Southern Vegetable Curry
GAENG LIANG

This curry paste is particular to this dish. It doesn't use many ingredients and is quick to make. White peppercorns have a milder taste than black ones.

left
Southern
Vegetable Curry

900ml water
110g courgettes, cut into 2.5cm cubes
110g pumpkin, cut into 2.5cm cubes
110g baby sweetcorn, sliced diagonally in half
110g oyster mushrooms, separated
2 medium tomatoes, quartered
20 sweet basil leaves

for the curry paste
1/2 teaspoon white peppercorns
4 small dried red chillies
1/2 teaspoon salt
6 small Thai shallots

First make the curry paste. Pound the peppercorns in a stone mortar to a powder, then add the chillies and pound again. Add the salt and shallots and pound the mixture into a paste.

Bring the water to the boil in a pan and stir in the curry paste. Add the vegetables, reduce the heat and simmer for 20 minutes, stirring occasionally. Add the basil leaves and serve.

Morning Glory and Mushrooms topped with Curry
PALAM LONGSONG

Morning glory, or water spinach has long stems and grows in the water. It looks like Western spinach and has a similar taste and texture. Unfortunately morning glory doesn't travel well because the leaves turn yellow quickly and drop off. Thankfully the Chinese love it so much that they now grow and sell it in the West.

225ml coconut milk
1 tablespoon Penang Curry Paste (see page 29)
2 tablespoons light soy sauce
1 tablespoon tamarind water
1 tablespoon palm sugar
2 tablespoons ground salted peanuts
450g morning glory, chopped into 5cm pieces
8 dried Chinese mushrooms, boiled in water
  for 20 minutes, drained and squeezed, stems
  removed, then thinly sliced

Gently heat the coconut milk in a pan, simmer for 5 minutes, stirring. Add the curry paste, stir, then add the soy sauce, tamarind water and sugar, stirring well. Bring to the boil, stir in the peanuts, cook for 1 minute, then set aside.

Bring a pan of water to the boil, blanch the morning glory until soft, then drain and place on a serving plate. Blanch the mushrooms quickly in the same pan to heat them through and place on top of the morning glory. Pour over the curry sauce and serve.

Pickled Bamboo Curry
GAENG SOM NORMAI

Pickled bamboo is available in jars from oriental stores. The bamboo is boiled and then pickled in vinegar, sugar and salt, giving it a sour taste. Bamboo grows very quickly in Asia so it is often preserved in this way. As with mushrooms, some varieties are poisonous so check first if you are tempted to try this yourself!

900ml water
2 tablespoons Orange Curry Paste (see page 31)
900g pickled bamboo shoots, thinly sliced
2 large fresh red chillies, finely sliced

Bring the water to the boil in a pan and stir in the curry paste. Reduce the heat, add the bamboo shoots and simmer for 20 minutes. Add the chillies, and serve.

Vegetarian Samosa in Crispy Tofu Cups
TAO HOU SAMOSA

The filling for this recipe makes enough to make about 30 cups, but you can store it in the fridge for up to 2 days if you don't need that quantity.

Oil, for deep-frying
240g soft tofu, cut into 5cm squares

for the filling
3 tablespoons oil
2 garlic cloves, finely chopped
1 medium potato, finely chopped
1 medium onion, finely chopped
1 medium carrot, finely chopped
Kernels from 1 sweetcorn
2 spring onions, finely chopped
1 tablespoon Curry Powder (see page 32)
1/2 teaspoon salt
1 teaspoon sugar
1/2 teaspoon ground black pepper

First make the filling. Heat the oil in a pan and fry the garlic until golden brown. Add the remaining ingredients in turn, stirring constantly, then cook for 5 minutes. Set aside.

Heat the oil in a wok and deep-fry the tofu until golden brown. Remove and drain on kitchen paper. Cut a little cross shape in the centre of each square and gently scoop a round dent into the piece to make a cup. Place a teaspoon of the filling inside, then serve.

Stir-fried Spicy Mixed Vegetables
GAENG BHAN PAK

2 tablespoons oil
2 garlic cloves, finely chopped
1 tablespoon Home-style Curry Paste
  (see page 31)
1 medium carrot, finely sliced
110g mangetout, trimmed
110g small straw mushrooms, halved
  lengthways
110g aubergines, cut into 3cm cubes
2 tablespoons light soy sauce
1 teaspoon sugar
20 sweet basil leaves

Heat the oil in a wok and fry the garlic until golden brown. Stir in the curry paste, then add the remaining ingredients. Stir-fry for 3–4 minutes, spoon into a dish and serve.

Papaya Curry
GAENG LUANG

This is a very hot curry from southern Thailand that is given its bright yellow colour by the fresh turmeric. Local people add yellow chillies to the sauce for extra heat and colour. It's usually made with prawns but this is my vegetarian version.

900ml water
900g green papaya, peeled, deseeded and cut into 3cm slices
1 tablespoon tamarind water
4 medium tomatoes, quartered
1 teaspoon salt

for the yellow curry paste
4 small dried red chillies
1/2 teaspoon salt
1 tablespoon finely chopped lemongrass
1 tablespoon finely chopped garlic
2 teaspoons finely chopped fresh turmeric

First make the curry paste. Pound the chillies in a stone mortar, then add the remaining ingredients, pounding each one in turn, until the mixture forms a paste.

Bring the water to the boil in a pan and stir in the curry paste. Add the papaya, tamarind water, tomatoes and salt and simmer for 20 minutes or until the papaya is soft, then serve.

UNRIPE PAPAYAS
Unripe papayas are treated like vegetables in Thailand. They have green skin and flesh and are used in hot dishes and salads, whereas ripe papayas have orange flesh and are eaten as fruit.

Stir-fried Spicy Cauliflower and Long Beans
PAD PET DOK GALAM

We Thais don't like our vegetables to be too soft. They should be quickly stir-fried to keep the texture crunchy. The cauliflower in particular should not be overcooked.

2 tablespoons oil
3 garlic cloves, finely chopped
1 tablespoon Red Curry Paste (see page 28)
450g cauliflower, cut into florets
125ml water
225g long beans, cut into 3cm lengths
2 tablespoons light soy sauce
1 teaspoon sugar
2 tablespoons lime juice

Heat the oil in a wok and fry the garlic until crispy, then remove and set aside. Stir the curry paste into the oil, then add the cauliflower and water and simmer for 3 minutes.

Add the beans, soy sauce and sugar and stir-fry for 2 minutes, stirring constantly. Stir in the lime juice, then transfer to a dish. Garnish with the crispy garlic and serve.

LONG BEANS
At up to a metre in length, the aptly named long bean resembles a wildly overgrown string bean (which can be used as a substitute). The long bean, however, is crunchier and cooks faster. Choose darker beans with small seeds inside the pods.

Vegetable Curry
GAENG PET PAK

This is very popular with vegetarians because of the mixture of tastes and textures.

left
Vegetable Curry

2 tablespoons oil
2 tablespoons Red Curry Paste (see page 28)
450ml coconut cream (see page 25)
450ml vegetable stock
6 long beans, cut into 2.5cm pieces
6 baby sweetcorn, cut into 2.5cm pieces
6 round Thai aubergines, quartered
1 large carrot, cut into matchsticks
2 large fresh red or green chillies, sliced
4 kaffir lime leaves, roughly chopped
2 teaspoons salt
2 teaspoons sugar
2 tablespoons light soy sauce
30 sweet basil leaves

Heat the oil in a pan and stir in the curry paste. Add the coconut cream, mixing well, then stir in the stock. Add all the vegetables, the lime leaves, salt, sugar and soy sauce. Stir well, then cook briefly until the vegetables are cooked to your taste. Ladle into a bowl, stir in the basil leaves and serve.

Stir-fried Spicy Baby Sweetcorn and Mushrooms
PAD KIMOW JAY

Baby sweetcorn have a wonderfully sweet fragrance and flavour and an irresistible texture. They are available both fresh and tinned.

3 tablespoons oil
1 tablespoon Home-style Curry Paste
  (see page 31)
225g baby sweetcorn, thickly sliced
175g oyster mushrooms, separated
2 stems of fresh green peppercorns
2 medium tomatoes, quartered
4 kaffir lime leaves, finely sliced
2 tablespoons light soy sauce
1 teaspoon sugar
2 tablespoons water
1 large fresh red chilli, thinly sliced

Heat the oil in a wok, stir in the curry paste, then add the remaining ingredients in turn, stirring constantly. Cook for 2 minutes, then transfer to a dish and serve.

Stuffed Omelette
MATABAK

This dish was originally a southern Thai Muslim speciality.

3 eggs
1 tablespoon light soy sauce
2 tablespoons oil

for the filling
2 tablespoons oil
2 teaspoons finely chopped garlic
50g onions, finely chopped
50g fresh or frozen peas
50g tomatoes, finely chopped
50g carrots, finely chopped
50g straw mushrooms, finely chopped
50g peppers, finely chopped
2 teaspoons Curry Powder (see page 32)
2 tablespoons light soy sauce
1/2 teaspoon sugar
1/2 teaspoon ground black pepper

First make the filling. Heat the oil in a pan and fry the garlic until golden. Add the remaining ingredients in turn, cooking for about 5–10 minutes and stirring constantly. Remove from the heat and set aside.

Beat the eggs, add the soy sauce and mix well. Heat the oil in a wok, tilting it to coat the entire surface with the oil.

Pour in the egg and tip the wok to spread evenly. When the egg has dried, pour the filling into the centre. Fold in the sides of the omelette to make a square parcel. Cook briefly to warm through the filling, then lift carefully onto a dish and serve.

right
Stuffed Omelette

Vegetable Curry with Pickled Garlic
GAENG PAK KRATIAM DONG

Pickled garlic is a powerful flavouring – whole heads of garlic are preserved in a rich, salty liquid (see page 98).

3 tablespoons oil
2 tablespoons Curry Powder (see page 32)
2 whole heads of Pickled Garlic, sliced
  (see page 34)
4 tablespoons water
175g mixed vegetables (carrots, beans,
  sweetcorn, celery), cut into small pieces
2 spring onions, chopped into 3cm lengths
1/2 teaspoon salt
1 tablespoon chopped fresh coriander

Heat the oil in a wok, stir in the curry powder, then add the remaining ingredients in turn, stirring constantly. Cook for 2–3 minutes, then transfer to a dish and serve, garnished with the coriander.

Pineapple Curry
GAENG KUA SAPPAROT

If you buy a pineapple and find it is too sour to eat on its own, this is a great way to use it and bring out the flavour.

left
Pineapple Curry

2 tablespoons oil
2 tablespoons Kua Curry Paste (see page 30)
450ml coconut cream (see page 25)
225ml water
2 tablespoons light soy sauce
1/2 teaspoon salt
2 tablespoons lime juice
4 kaffir lime leaves, thinly sliced
**1 fresh pineapple, trimmed and cut into
    small cubes**
Finely chopped red chilli, for garnish

Heat the oil in a pan and fry the curry paste, stirring well. Stir in the coconut cream. Add the water, slowly bring to the boil, then add the soy sauce, salt, lime juice, lime leaves and pineapple. Simmer for 3 minutes, then transfer to a bowl, garnish with chilli and serve.

Spicy Mushroom Curry
HET PAD PET

This is a great dish for vegetarians because mushrooms have a mealy, satisfying texture. Use a mixture such as chestnut, oyster and other wild mushrooms.

225ml coconut cream (see page 25)
450g mixed mushrooms, chopped
1 tablespoon Orange Curry Paste (see page 31)
2 tablespoons light soy sauce
1 teaspoon sugar
1 tablespoon finely sliced *krachai* (see page 23)
1 large fresh red chilli, finely sliced
20 basil leaves

Gently heat the coconut cream in a pan, stirring well for 2 minutes. Add the mushrooms, cook for 2 minutes, then stir in the remaining ingredients in turn, and cook for a further 2 minutes. Transfer to a dish and serve.

Stir-fried Aubergines with Green Curry Paste and Bean Sauce
MAKUA PAT KEOW WAN

This curry can be made with any aubergines, the common large purple ones as seen on the right or Thai aubergines as below. If the purple ones are used they should be cooked until soft, whereas Thai aubergines are better left al dente.

2 tablespoons oil
2 tablespoons Green Curry Paste (see page 28)
450g aubergines, cut into 2.5cm cubes
4 tablespoons vegetable stock or water
75g red pepper, cored, deseeded and cut
  lengthways into thin strips
1 tablespoon bean sauce
1 tablespoon light soy sauce
1 tablespoon sugar
2 large fresh red chillies, thinly sliced
20 holy basil leaves

Heat the oil in a pan and stir in the curry paste. Stir in the aubergine and stock, and cook until the aubergine begins to soften (about 5 minutes). Add the remaining ingredients, stirring constantly. Cook for 1 minute and serve.

AUBERGINES
The purple-black aubergine common in the West is used in Thai cooking, along with several other less familiar varieties. The Thai aubergine most commonly available in oriental supermarkets is round, pale green and about 2.5cm in diameter (as seen left). The smaller Thai pea aubergine is generally rarer outside Thailand and tastes more bitter (see picture on page 12).

Chickpea Curry
GAENG PET TUA

Chickpeas are not commonly used in Thai cooking – this dish shows its Indian roots.

2 tablespoons oil
2 tablespoons Massaman Curry Paste
  (see page 29)
450ml coconut cream (see page 25)
450ml water
2 medium potatoes, peeled and cut into
  2.5cm cubes
225g dried chickpeas, soaked overnight,
  or use tinned
2 small onions, cut into 2.5cm cubes
2 large fresh red chillies, cut lengthways into
  thin slivers
2 tablespoons light soy sauce
1/2 teaspoon salt
1 tablespoon sugar

Heat the oil in a pan and stir in the curry paste. Stir in the coconut cream, mixing well, then add the remaining ingredients in turn.

Bring to the boil and simmer for about 15 minutes until the potatoes and chickpeas are cooked. Transfer to a dish and serve.

Tofu and Ginger Curry
KARI TAO HOU

Tofu is an ingredient that came to Thailand with the Chinese. Putting tofu into an Indian-style curry is a good example of how Thai food has fused elements of Chinese and Indian cooking.

Oil, for deep-frying
450g tofu, cut into 2.5cm cubes
2 tablespoons oil
2 tablespoons Curry Powder (see page 32)
225ml coconut cream (see page 25)
2 tablespoons light soy sauce
1 tablespoon tamarind water
1 teaspoon sugar
3 tablespoons water
1 tablespoon finely sliced ginger

Heat the oil in a wok and deep-fry the tofu until golden brown on all sides. Drain on kitchen paper and set aside.

Heat the 2 tablespoons of oil in a second wok and stir in the curry powder. Add the remaining ingredients in turn, stirring constantly, and cook for 2 minutes. Stir in the fried tofu, cook for a further 2 minutes, then serve.

Green Curry with Young Coconut
GAENG KEOW WAN MAPROW

You can find young green coconuts (see below) in oriental stores and they are also available tinned. You need two young green coconuts for this recipe. Cut them open, drain off the coconut water (a refreshing drink when chilled) and use the coconut flesh. Traditionally this curry is served inside the coconut shell.

2 tablespoons oil
2 garlic cloves, finely chopped
2 tablespoons Green Curry Paste (see page 28)
450ml coconut cream (see page 25)
450ml water
175g young coconut flesh, thinly sliced (see above)
2 large fresh red chillies, sliced diagonally into thin ovals
1 teaspoon salt
8 round Thai aubergines, quartered
2 teaspoons sugar
20 sweet basil leaves

Heat the oil in a large pan, add the garlic and fry until golden brown. Stir in the curry paste, mixing well. Add the coconut cream and keep stirring for 2 minutes.

Slowly add the water and bring to the boil, stirring constantly. Add the sliced coconut, chillies, salt, aubergines and sugar. Simmer for about 3 minutes until the aubergines are cooked. Stir in the basil leaves just before pouring into a bowl and serve.

Boiled Egg Curry
GAENG KAI

Makes a good breakfast or lunch dish.

2 tablespoons oil
5 small shallots, finely sliced
3 garlic cloves, finely sliced
2 tablespoons Massaman Curry Paste
  (see page 29)
125ml water
3 cardamom pods
5 cloves
5cm piece of cinnamon stick
125ml coconut milk
2 teaspoons salt
1 tablespoon palm sugar
6 hard-boiled eggs, peeled and halved
2 large fresh red chillies, sliced

for the garnish
1 tablespoon deep-fried onions
2 large fresh red chillies, finely sliced
Coriander leaves

Heat the oil in a pan and fry the shallots and garlic for 2 minutes. Stir in the curry paste, mixing well. Add the water and the remaining ingredients in turn. Simmer gently for 10 minutes. Garnish with the deep-fried onions, chillies and coriander leaves, and serve.

Conversion Table

Weight (solids)

7g	$\frac{1}{4}$oz
10g	$\frac{1}{2}$oz
20g	$\frac{3}{4}$oz
25g	1oz
40g	1$\frac{1}{2}$oz
50g	2oz
60g	2$\frac{1}{2}$oz
75g	3oz
100g	3$\frac{1}{2}$oz
110g	4oz ($\frac{1}{4}$lb)
125g	4$\frac{1}{2}$oz
150g	5$\frac{1}{2}$oz
175g	6oz
200g	7oz
225g	8oz ($\frac{1}{2}$lb)
250g	9oz
275g	10oz
300g	10$\frac{1}{2}$oz
310g	11oz
325g	11$\frac{1}{2}$oz
350g	12oz ($\frac{3}{4}$lb)
375g	13oz
400g	14oz
425g	15oz
450g	1lb
500g ($\frac{1}{2}$kg)	18oz
600g	1$\frac{1}{4}$lb
700g	1$\frac{1}{2}$lb
750g	1lb 10oz
900g	2lb
1kg	2$\frac{1}{4}$lb
1.1kg	2$\frac{1}{2}$lb
1.2kg	2lb 12oz
1.3kg	3lb
1.5kg	3lb 5oz
1.6kg	3$\frac{1}{2}$lb
1.8kg	4lb
2kg	4lb 8oz
2.25kg	5lb
2.5kg	5lb 8oz
3kg	6lb 8oz

Volume (liquids)

5ml	1 teaspoon
10ml	1 dessertspoon
15ml	1 tablespoon or $\frac{1}{2}$fl oz
30ml	1fl oz
40ml	1$\frac{1}{2}$fl oz
50ml	2fl oz
60ml	2$\frac{1}{2}$fl oz
75ml	3fl oz
100ml	3$\frac{1}{2}$fl oz
125ml	4fl oz
150ml	5fl oz ($\frac{1}{4}$ pint)
160ml	5$\frac{1}{2}$fl oz
175ml	6fl oz
200ml	7fl oz
225ml	8fl oz
250ml (0.25 litre)	9fl oz
300ml	10fl oz ($\frac{1}{2}$ pint)
325ml	11fl oz
350ml	12fl oz
370ml	13fl oz
400ml	14fl oz
425ml	15fl oz ($\frac{3}{4}$ pint)
450ml	16fl oz
500ml (0.5 litre)	18fl oz
550ml	19fl oz
600ml	20fl oz (1 pint)
700ml	1$\frac{1}{4}$ pints
850ml	1$\frac{1}{2}$ pints
1 litre	1$\frac{3}{4}$ pints
1.2 litres	2 pints
1.5 litres	2$\frac{1}{2}$ pints
1.8 litres	3 pints
2 litres	3$\frac{1}{2}$ pints

Length

5mm	$\frac{1}{4}$in
1cm	$\frac{1}{2}$in
2cm	$\frac{3}{4}$in
2.5cm	1in
3cm	1$\frac{1}{4}$in
4cm	1$\frac{1}{2}$in
5cm	2in
7.5cm	3in
10cm	4in
15cm	6in
18cm	7in
20cm	8in
24cm	10in
28cm	11in
30cm	12in

Oven temperatures

CELSIUS*	FAHRENHEIT	GAS	DESCRIPTION
110 C	225 F	mark $\frac{1}{4}$	cool
130 C	250 F	mark $\frac{1}{2}$	cool
140 C	275 F	mark 1	very low
150 C	300 F	mark 2	very low
170 C	325 F	mark 3	low
180 C	350 F	mark 4	moderate
190 C	375 F	mark 5	mod. hot
200 C	400 F	mark 6	hot
220 C	425 F	mark 7	hot
230 C	450 F	mark 8	very hot

*For fan-assisted ovens, reduce temperatures by 10°C

Index

ab ong nua 117
accompaniments 32
ajart 34
aubergines 10, 102, 164
    stir-fried aubergines with green curry paste and bean sauce 164

ba mee siam 58
bamboo 76, 130
    pickled bamboo curry 152
banana 72, 79, 134
basil 16
bean sauce (*tow jiew*) 25
beans 105, 156, 164
beef 12
    beef curry from Pattani 110
    curry flavoured beef noodles 52
    dry beef curry 110
    green curry with beef 114
    grilled beef curry with figs 113
    hot dry beef curry 113
    northern barbecued minced beef patty 117
    spicy beef balls 51
    stir-fried beef noodles with curry paste 52
bet grob 89
bet kari 90
bet keow wan 90
bitter melon curry 106
boo pad pet 142
boo pad pong kari 142

cardamom 22
cauliflower and long bean spicy stir-fry 156
chicken
    black pepper chicken curry 75
    chicken and lime curry 72
    chicken curry with green banana 72
    chicken curry with sour bamboo shoots 76
    chicken fried rice with green curry paste 63
    chicken massaman curry 80
    chicken Penang 68
    fried sweet potato and chicken cakes 43
    noodles with chicken, pork and prawns 58
    north-eastern steamed chicken curry in banana leaf 79
    northern chicken curry 76
    southern chicken curry 71
    spicy roast chicken 68
    spicy stuffed roast chicken 80
    tamarind chicken 83
chickpea curry 167
chillies 16, 22, 142

chu chee pla 126
cinnamon 22
clove 22
coconut 147
    coconut and vegetable curry 148
    coconut milk 25
    curry coconut rice 60
    green curry with young coconut 168
    prawn and coconut cakes with plum sauce 44
    spicy coconut cakes 43
    spicy coconut chicken 71
cooking curry 20
coriander 15, 22
crab 56
    chilli crab 142
    crab with curry powder 142
curry pastes 11, 48, 52
    ingredients 22–25
    making 26
    recipes 28–31

drink 33
duck
    crispy duck with curry sauce 89
    duck curry 90
    hot duck curry 88
    roast duck with lychee curry 87
    roasted duck with green curry paste 90

eggs 141
    boiled egg curry 171
    salted eggs 34
    stuffed omelette 160

figs with grilled beef curry 113
fish 10, 12
    curried fish balls with bamboo shoots 130
    fish curry with kaffir lime 125
    fish curry with papaya 129
    fish sauce (*nam pla*) 24–25
    grilled curried fish 122
    haddock with green curry sauce 125
    mackerel in red curry 126
    sea bass with curry sauce 129
    southern Thai fish curry 122

gadook moo yang 101
gaeng bhan 31
gaeng bhan moo pa 109
gaeng bhan pak 153
gaeng bet yang 87
gaeng daeng moo 101

gaeng gai chiang rai 76
gaeng gai kloi 72
gaeng gai ma-now 72
gaeng gai normai dong 76
gaeng gai prik thai dum 75
gaeng hoh 109
gaeng hung lay 98
gaeng kachiap kaek 114
gaeng kai 171
gaeng keow wan 28
gaeng keow wan maprow 168
gaeng keow wan nua 114
gaeng kua 30
gaeng kua hoy 138
gaeng kua sapparot 163
gaeng liang 151
gaeng luang 155
gaeng madua nua yang 113
gaeng man gap het 148
gaeng marak 106
gaeng massaman 29
gaeng massaman gai 80
gaeng nua Pattani 110
gaeng nua yala 110
gaeng pa 30
gaeng pa lukchin pla 130
gaeng pak kratiam dong 160
gaeng pet bet 88
gaeng pet moo faengtong 96
gaeng pet pak 159
gaeng pet pla 122
gaeng pet tua 167
gaeng pet jay 148
gaeng Penang 29
gaeng pet 28
gaeng pla makrut 125
gaeng som 31, 152
gai kelek 71
gai krati 71
gai makham 83
gai ob 68
gai sot sai 80
galangal 23
garlic 15, 23, 34, 98, 160
ginger 23, 34, 167
green curry paste 28, 63, 102, 164
gueyteow gaeng jay 51
gueyteow kaek 56
gueyteow nua sap 52

haw mok kung 134
haw nung gai 79
het pad pet 163
home-style curry paste 31
holy basil 16

jungle curry paste 30

kaffir lime 23, 125
kai kem 34
kanom pang talay 47
kari pla muk 137, 141
kari tao hou 167
keow wan pla 125
khao garee kai 60
khao pad keow wan gai 63
khao pad pong kari kung 60
king dong 34
kow mok kaek 59
kow pad jay 59
krachai (chinesekey) 23
kratiam dong 35
kua curry paste 30
kua haeng si krong moo 105

lamb and okra curry 114
lamb curry with rice 59
lamb massaman curry 117
lemongrass 15, 23
lime 10
    chicken and lime curry 72
    fish curry with kaffir lime 125
long beans 156
lychee curry 87

massaman curry paste 29
massaman kaek 117
matabak 160
meat 94–95
    northern mixed meat curry 109
mee krop 55
mee pad boo 56
mee sua 52
mok hoy 63
moo pad prik king 105
moo pad makua 102
moo Penang 99
moo satay 40
morning glory and mushrooms topped with curry
    151
mushrooms 148, 151, 159
    spicy mushroom curry 163
mussels stuffed with curry 63
mussels with pineapple curry 138

nok ping 84
nok tod 84
noodles 32, 52
    noodles with chicken, pork and prawns 58
    noodles with curry sauce 51
    southern curry noodles 56

spicy crispy noodles 55
   Thai fried noodles with crab 56
nua kua klink 113
nua tod 51
nutmeg 23
okra and lamb curry 114
orange curry paste 31

pad cha kung 137
pad kimow jay 159
pad pad talay 133
pad pet dok galam 156
pad pet kung 133
pad pet pla muk 141
pak chup bang tod 48
palam longsong 151
papaya 155
papaya curry 155
pat pet moo 99
peanut curry sauce with pork satay 40
Penang curry paste 29
Penang gai 68
Penang kung 134
peppercorn 23, 75
pheasant, fried crispy 84
pickles 34–35, 98, 152, 160
pineapple curry 138, 163
pla gaeng som 129
pla lad prik 129
pla muk korleh 126
pla yang prik gaeng 122
plum sauce 44
pork 12
   fried pork curry 99
   noodles with chicken, pork and prawns 58
   pork curry with pickled garlic 98
   pork in red curry with pumpkin 96
   pork Penang curry 99
   pork red curry 101
   pork satay with peanut curry sauce 40
   roast spicy pork chops 101
   spare ribs with bitter melon curry 106
   spicy pork with long beans 105
   spicy spare ribs 105
   stir-fried minced pork with aubergine and green
      curry paste 102
   wild boar curry 109
prawns 58
   fried curried rice with prawns 60
   prawn and coconut cakes with plum sauce 44
   prawn curry 134
   spicy prawns with peppercorns 137
   steamed prawn curry in banana leaf 134
   stir-fry prawn curry 133
pumpkin with pork in red curry 96

quail, barbecued spicy 84

red curry paste 28
rice 9, 10, 12, 32, 59, 60, 66–67
   chicken fried rice with green curry paste 63

seafood, spicy stir-fried 133
seafood toast 47
servings and quantities 9
shallots 23
shrimp paste (*kapee*) 17, 23
soy sauce (*siew*) 25
squid
   barbecued curried squid 126
   spicy squid 141
   squid curry with salted eggs 141
   squid curry 137
star anise 23
stock 25
sweet basil 16
sweet potato and chicken cakes 43
sweet potato and mushroom curry 148
sweetcorn and mushroom stir-fry 159
sweetcorn cakes 44

tamarind 23
   tamarind chicken 83
tamarind water 83
tao hou samosa 153
taro 48
Thailand 9–10
   cuisine 11–13, 15–17
   regional differences 19
tod man gai 43
tod man khao pod 44
tod man kung 44
tod man maprao 43
tofu 153
turmeric 23
   tofu and ginger curry 167

vegetables 10, 11, 12, 147
   coconut and vegetable curry 148
   fresh vegetable pickle 34
   southern vegetable curry 151
   stir-fried spicy mixed vegetables 153
   vegetable curry 159
   vegetable curry with pickled garlic 160
   vegetable fritters with curry paste 48
   vegetarian fried rice 59
   vegetarian samosa in crispy tofu cups 153